SOCIAL SCIENCE SEMINAR SERIES

Raymond H. Muessig and Vincent R. Rogers, Editors

THE VOLUMES AND THE AUTHORS

The Study of Anthropology, Pertti J. Pelto

Political Science: An Informal Overview, Francis J. Sorauf

Geography: Its Scope and Spirit, Jan O. M. Broek

Sociology: The Study of Man in Society, Caroline B. Rose

The Nature and the Study of History, Henry Steele Commager

Economics and Its Significance, Richard S. Martin and
  Reuben G. Miller

THE CONSULTANTS FOR THE SERIES

Anthropology, George D. Spindler

Political Science, Charles S. Hyneman

Geography, Jan O. M. Broek

Sociology, Arnold M. Rose

History, Henry Steele Commager

Economics, Kenneth E. Boulding

POLITICAL SCIENCE

AN INFORMAL OVERVIEW

Francis J. Sorauf
Department of Political Science
University of Minnesota

Charles S. Hyneman, *Consultant*
Department of Government
Indiana University

*With a Concluding Chapter Suggesting Methods
for Elementary and Secondary Teachers
by* **Raymond H. Muessig** *and* **Vincent R. Rogers**

CHARLES E. MERRILL BOOKS, INC.   COLUMBUS, OHIO

Library of Congress Catalog Card Number: 65–21163

First printing ....June, 1965
Second printing ....March, 1966

Social Science Seminar Series

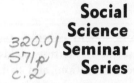

Edited by Raymond H. Muessig
and Vincent R. Rogers

The Social Science Seminar Series presents scholarly viewpoints on and information about history, geography, political science, economics, sociology, and anthropology. This social science material is complemented by creative and practical methods, tailored to each of the individual fields, for elementary and secondary teachers.

One assumption built into these six volumes is that the social studies program in our schools should reflect more faithfully and sensitively the social sciences from which it is derived. It is imperative, then, that social scientists contribute their suggestions regarding over-all content selection problems in the social studies.

A second premise inherent in the Social Science Seminar Series is that professional educators are responsible for translating appropriate social science substance into meaningful and enriching learning experiences for children and youth. In their contacts with the editors of this Series, the contributing social scientists repeatedly made the point that they could discuss their disciplines only as they saw them and not in the light of what should be done with them in the schools. It is the professional educator—thoroughly prepared and broadly experienced in thinking about and coping with educational theories, problems, and practices—who must weld a framework that will support understandings, skills, attitudes, and appreciations drawn from or tied to the social science disciplines. It is the educator, too, who must decide what can and should be taught at various grade levels and how this subject matter might be conveyed, buttressed, and assessed by a myriad of suitable methods, materials, resources, and evaluative processes.

There is a critical need in both pre-service and in-service teacher education programs for up-to-date, clear, stimulating material concerned with recent developments in the social sciences. Teachers should see these disciplines as spheres of continuing scientific study and inquiry, rather than as hardened, static, sterile bodies of accumulated fact. Further, they must obtain a more sophisticated grasp of the goals, scope, importance, and interpretation of these fields as well as some understanding of the concerns faced by those working in a given field. The Social Science Seminar Series encourages and assists teachers at all instructional levels to critically examine their purposes and approaches to the teaching of specific areas of content fundamentally related to the disciplines treated.

With this perspective in mind, the editors of the Series suggested that each of the contributing social scientists ask himself what his field really does contain that professional educators should consider teaching to youngsters. Each author was asked to describe the nature of his field; to trace briefly its history, development, and maturation; and to look at its unique methods of working as well as those procedures shared with other social sciences and related fields. Most importantly, each specialist was requested to select out of mountains of data a series of fundamental, compelling ideas that have emerged from his field.

In each volume of the Social Science Seminar Series, the editors have written a final chapter to accompany the discussions and analyses of the social scientists. The editors have *not* attempted to build an overarching theory of social studies education; rather, they have concentrated upon specific, functional classroom methods. The concluding chapters in this Series, therefore, do not present a total program, a master theory, a blanket plan of attack, or an endorsement of the proposals of any single group endeavoring to improve social studies instruction. The generalizations the editors have chosen to illustrate should not be viewed as the basis for a course or sequence of offerings. The ideas they have introduced transcend particular topics, units, themes, or curricula. Careful exposure to them can support many learnings. The editors have not dealt at this time with *why, how much, where,* and *when* questions regarding the place of individual social sciences in the social studies family today or tomorrow. As they see it, each social science can be taught by itself in breadth or depth, woven into existing scope and sequence patterns for development or supplementary purposes, or assigned manifold roles in some yet-to-be-developed curriculum design.

Space limitations have not permitted the exhaustive treatment of a single idea, problem, or approach drawn from each of the social sciences represented. Instead, the editors have suggested a number of procedures that could be used or adapted for use in a variety of elementary and secondary school situations. It is not intended that the techniques offered in the Series be employed in a one-a-day, isolated, disjointed, decontextualized fashion. A superficial flitting from one major insight to another would have little meaning for students and would possess limited retention or transfer value. It is not expected that pupils will comprehend abstract generalizations in a definitive sense after an occasional lesson or two. The editors believe that global ideas should be approached, discovered, introduced, developed, and confirmed in different ways and contexts and at increased levels of complexity throughout the school years. They have taken into account the fact that it takes time, patience, and systematic organization to build durable learning.

The Social Science Seminar Series, then, should function as a point of embarkation—inspiring and challenging readers to keep abreast of developments in the social sciences and in social studies education.

Preface

John Haynes Holmes once warned .that "the life of humanity upon this planet may yet come to . . . a very terrible end. But I would have you notice that this end is threatened in our time not by anything that the universe may do to us but only by what man may do to himself." It is largely in this context that the youthful science of politics takes on vital new meanings for twentieth-century man. Every known society, no matter how advanced or retarded its technology, no matter how central or isolated its physical location, no matter how spiritual or material its system of values, must arrive at what the political scientist calls "authoritative policy." Decisions must be made; goals must be implemented. Each society is inextricably bound up, however, in the ultimate political goals and policies decided upon and carried out by its neighbors. What happens in a newly organized African state *does* matter to the citizens of the United States, as it does to citizens of the Soviet Union. Similarly, political decisions made in the United States and in the Soviet Union may affect the very existence of a host of other nations. The study of political science offers us an opportunity to understand the fundamental nature of the political process, and it seems that nothing could be of greater significance to the citizens of a rapidly changing, increasingly interdependent world.

This book is the culmination of the extended, cooperative efforts of a political scientist and two social studies educators. The first five chapters, on the field itself, were written by Dr. Francis J. Sorauf of the Department of Political Science at the University of Minnesota. Dr. Sorauf deals with the birth and growth of political science, its current problems, emphases, theories, and findings as well as the methods and techniques utilized by the practicing political scientist. The reader will find that Dr. Sorauf has also recommended numerous sources for independent study which should be both stimulating and enriching. The last chapter, on classroom methodology, was written by Dr. Raymond H. Muessig of the College of Education at The Ohio State University and Dr. Vincent R. Rogers of the College of Education at the University of Minnesota. Focusing on a group of basic insights drawn from Dr. Sorauf's preceding chapters, Dr. Muessig and Dr. Rogers propose and illustrate numerous approaches that teachers might employ to help elementary and secondary school students gain some understanding of these important insights and observations of political science. Dr. Charles S. Hyneman of the Department of Government at Indiana University served as academic consultant for this volume.

The Editors

Table
of
Contents

POLITICAL SCIENCE
AN INFORMAL OVERVIEW

The
Political and
the Nonpolitical

chapter one

As all but one member of the United States Senate trooped in to vote September 24, 1963, on the nuclear test ban treaty, ratification was a foregone conclusion. The debate that had raged both in and out of the Senate since the signing of the treaty in Moscow on the fifth of August had been effectively settled some days earlier when President John F. Kennedy won over reluctant Republican leadership with the assurance that the treaty was not a renunciation of nuclear weapons for defensive purposes.

The eighty-to-nineteen vote for ratification only capped a series of events which had begun with President Kennedy's early attempts to ease Cold War tensions and, more immediately, with the negotiation and signing of the treaty. Within the seven-week period between signing and ratification the President and his administration, American friends and allies abroad, powerful interest groups and spokesmen in the mass media, party notables and senatorial leaders, influential Americans and citizens not so influential, former Presidents, and letter-to-the-editor authors had directed an intensive, unremitting stream of influence at the Senate in support for and opposition to the treaty. Senators were deluged by letters from constituents, by attention from the White House, and by the entreaties of other senators. Predictions of the dire consequences of signing the treaty were pitted against predictions of the equally disastrous consequences of not signing it.

Such dramatic public encounters over the setting of American foreign or domestic policy involve events, officials, and institutions which both the informed layman and the political scientist would call political. They are focal points at which all of the complicated,

1

interrelated political processes in the American society converge. All of these processes, of course, take place within a formal arena or context defined by the American constitution—in the case of the test ban treaty within the separation of powers that divided the President from the Senate, within the constitutional proviso that treaties be ratified by an extraordinary two-thirds majority, and within the constitutional responsibility of the President for setting American foreign policy. The struggle over the test ban treaty, in other words, may be viewed as a massive attempt to influence and shape the setting of American foreign policy within the limits and bounds set by the formal apparatus of American political institutions.

Yet, debates and decisions such as this one are not isolated eruptions of the political process. They are related to other decisions and other political processes of the same time, and they also have consequences for future activity and decisions in the political system. The test ban treaty was one highly important part of a many-sectored American defense and foreign policy. Could the United States ratify the treaty without reconsidering and altering its defense strategies and particularly its dependence on nuclear deterrent power? Could it decline to ratify the treaty without sacrificing the support of allies and neutral nations and without outraging something we rather nebulously call world public opinion? The ramifications, both present and future, were not, however, limited to defense and foreign policy. A young President had staked a substantial share of his popularity and his political prospects for 1964 on relaxing tensions with the Soviet Union; and one of his possible opponents in 1964, Republican Senator Barry Goldwater, had gambled his chances for his party's nomination on an unyielding opposition to the treaty.

Common sense and daily usage indicate that this stream of activity and decisions involves government and politics. Political scientists would agree. These are obviously matters which they study and consider within the academic discipline of political science. The major problem the political scientist faces, however, in describing his study occurs when he moves from a particular case to a comprehensive, systematic definition of the scope of political science. He may casually define political science as the study of political behavior, processes, and institutions, or as the study of political systems and the relationships among them. Those brief formulas, however, beg the essential question: What do we mean by *politics* and the *political*? Popular usage offers little help, for Americans use the terms in a variety of ways. For some they refer merely to the activity of political parties and their adherents, a meaning which political scientists would prefer to assign to the word *partisan*. For others *politics* refers to any form or display of influence—academic politics, office politics, and PTA politics. That meaning most political scientists would reject as too loose, broad, and inclusive. But to say that the meaning of the concept lies somewhere in between these two definitions is one thing; to find it is another.

The task is clear, and it is challenging. How does one separate political behavior from nonpolitical behavior? When are the American Medical Association and the AFL-CIO engaged in politics and when are they not? In every society individuals and groups disagree over goals and directions for the society, over how the society will achieve the goals and provide services, over the definition and enforcement of standards of behavior; and every society has a number of institutions which settle these disagreements. At the trivial level, arbiters of etiquette and social usage may set and enforce certain social norms; for the untutored who misuse the oyster fork, their sanction is the withdrawal of social approval and the scorn of the "refined." More significantly, religious groups, ethnic associations, trade unions and corporations, family and kinship groups, and even fraternal associations determine goals and behavior for their members. One can, in fact, imagine a rough hierarchy of these arbitrative, goal-setting systems, the ones at the top having broader coverage and more potent enforcement power than those below them. The system of social control at the top of the hierarchy we call the political system.

As its peak the political system is marked by two distinctive characteristics: its universality and its finality of force. First, it alone extends to all people in the society; other agencies, such as religions and occupational associations, reach only a fraction of the whole. The political system possesses, secondly, a finality, and ultimately a monopoly, of coercive force in the society. It monopolizes organized armed force and the sanctions of imprisonment and death. Because it tops the hierarchy of authorities it can, indeed, set limits to coercion in systems below it. Even the power of religious groups in the United States to control the behavior of their members, should the groups' beliefs run to polygamy or snake-handling, may be limited by the ultimate sanctions of the political system.

Additionally, the political system enjoys what political scientists have for centuries called legitimacy. It enjoys an acceptance by the people of the society as the final authority, as a matter of custom, morality, or legality—or all three. Out of their loyalty to it they enforce its decisions on themselves and free the political system from the impossible task of supporting every one of its decisions with naked force. Men accept and give loyalty to other groups and associations, however. Their loyalty to the political system differs only in that it is usually stronger and concedes to it a greater coercive power in their lives.

Two of the most influential recent definitions of political science —those of David Easton and Harold Lasswell—indicate similar approaches to the political system. Easton describes the political system as the complex of processes and institutions which make "the authoritative allocation of values in society." [1] The operative word here, of course, is *authoritative*, for it sets the political above the other allocative systems. The Easton formulation sees the political system as the interrelationships by which men decide which competing goals and aspirations will be written into public policy and thus enforced in society. For Harold Lasswell this allocative system can be better understood by examining the power and influence of participants in it, by examining the ability of people to affect the allocation. In the mid-1930's he entitled one of his most influential books *Politics: Who Gets What, When and How.*[2]

The particularly careful reader may have noticed that the definitions of the last few paragraphs have not once referred to government, and he may have wondered why one cannot define the business of political science in terms of government. He would have on his side the argument that departments of political science in American colleges and universities are increasingly calling themselves departments of government. Nonetheless, there are two reasons for an unwillingness to treat government and politics synonymously. In the first place, it is only in certain political systems, most especially those of the Western democracies, that special institutions of government exist to perform only the political functions. That specialization does not exist in some political systems in which family, tribal, or kinship groups perform the political function in addition to their other social responsibilities.

Secondly, the institutions of government at best account for only part of the activity and part of the decisions in the political system. The political behavior of the individual, the operation of political parties and interest groups, the political power of individuals, elites, and the mass media—all these develop apart and aside from the institutions of government. Indeed, effective, final political power may be exercised outside of the institutions of government. Govern-

---

[1] David Easton, *The Political System* (New York: Alfred A. Knopf, Inc., 1953), chap. 5.

[2] New York: McGraw-Hill Book Co., 1936.

mental agencies in the Soviet Union exist only as automatic ratifiers of decisions reached within the ruling elite of the Communist party. In some corners of small-town America the city council or school board may only somewhat less automatically ratify decisions made by the town's leading citizens in informal consultations or over lunch at the local hotel.

Political science, then, studies this political system and, where they exist, the institutions of government around which it centers. It is concerned with the authoritative decision-making of the political system and with all of the processes and activities by which a society makes those decisions, chooses men to make them, and influences those who have been chosen. Its concern ranges from the individual's political interests and awareness to the complex operation of large political institutions. Its prime focus is on the processes of policy-making in the political system and on any activity that attempts to influence it. Any behavior concerned with those processes is political. To return to an earlier illustration, the American Medical Association and the AFL-CIO become engaged in political activity when they attempt to alter or reinforce the political views of their members, when they decide to seek their goals through the political system, or when they attempt political influence by means such as distributing political literature, aiding candidates for office, or testifying at legislative committee hearings.[3]

What we have been calling the political system may also be viewed (Figure 1) as a series of consecutive activities which culminate in the making of authoritative, binding decisions ("public policy"). Some of them take place within the formal institutions of government, and some do not. As Figure 1 suggests, it is a process by which individuals whose political goals and values have only insignificant political power are grouped together with other individuals into increasingly powerful aggregates in order to influence the making and applying of public policy. On the maker of public policy are concentrated the influences of his friends and associates, his constituents or clienteles, important political parties and interest groups, powerful elites and individuals, his fellow decision-makers, other

---

[3] The reader may also find it helpful in defining the scope of the political and the political system to consult: Robert A. Dahl, *Modern Political Analysis* (Englewood Cliffs, N.J.: Prentice-Hall, Inc., 1963) and Charles S. Hyneman, *The Study of Politics* (Urbana: University of Illinois Press, 1959). For an approach to the political through definitions of *the state*, see texts such as Dell G. Hitchner and William H. Harbold, *Modern Government* (New York: Dodd, Mead & Co., 1962). Chapter 4 of Easton's *The Political System* contains a valuable critique of that approach.

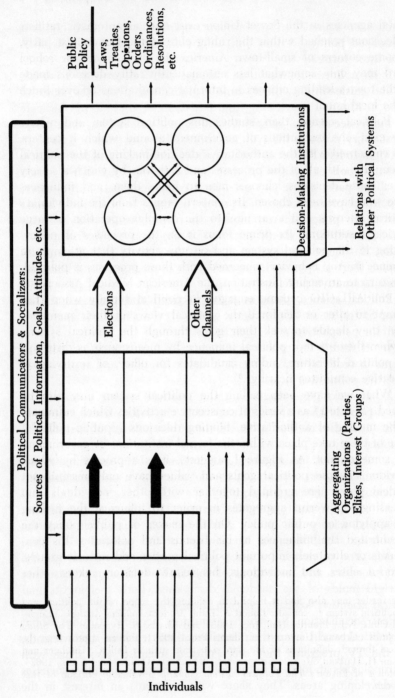

Figure 1. The Political System

Individuals

Public Policy

Laws,
Treaties,
Opinions,
Orders,
Ordinances,
Resolutions,
etc.

Decision-Making Institutions

Relations with
Other Political Systems

Elections

Other Channels

Aggregating
Organizations (Parties,
Elites, Interest Groups)

Political Communicators & Socializers:
Sources of Political Information, Goals, Attitudes, etc.

branches or agencies of government, opinion-makers, and his own internalized political values and judgments. Political influence takes all of these forms.

Such a linear representation of the political process, however, may be misleading without some qualification. Since the lines of action in Figure 1 move only from left to right, they do not indicate the many secondary, reciprocal influences within the system. At almost every point in the political process lines of influence also run from right to left. Parties and other political organizations, for instance, shape the political values of their members, and legislative action may shape party policy and even limit party activities. Furthermore, the political process cannot accurately be thought of in these linear terms. Since policy has an impact on future events and behavior within the system, it should also be thought of as a circular process. Finally, the figure derives largely from democratic political systems in which there is open and free mobilization of support and influence behind alternative policies.

Political science, then, as it is practiced and professed in the United States, studies this political system. It examines it, furthermore, from four perspectives:

1. It studies the processes, behavior, and institutions of political systems in order to make systematic generalizations and explanations about the political.

2. It seeks generalizations about relations among political systems, especially the politics of nations in the international system.

3. It studies the end products, the public policies, of the political processes.

4. It studies, finally, ideas and doctrines about government and the political system, ideas such as the concepts of and justifications for democracy, justice, and equality.

All of this is not to suggest, however, that the outer peripheries of political science are clearly staked out and fenced off from the neighboring social sciences. No concept of the political will define the discipline of political science with complete exactitude, for the social processes and institutions of the real world are not cast into the rigid molds of the academic disciplines. Both sociologists and political scientists logically concern themselves with the processes of political socialization by which youngsters acquire attitudes about the political world from their families, their teachers, their friends, and the TV programs they see. Political scientists also share with anthropologists an interest in the political systems of primitive societies and developing areas. They share with historians an interest in the political events of the past and with political geographers an interest in the bases of national power.

To complicate the issue further, political scientists are not themselves agreed on the outer limits of their discipline. They have in recent years disagreed on the extent to which they must make themselves experts in the substance of public policy—are they to organize knowledge about atomic energy and nuclear disarmament, about farm surpluses and water resources, foreign policy and military strategy, tariff agreements and management of the economy? Disagreement exists also on the extent to which they should be concerned with organizations that function politically only part of the time. Should their study of the political activities of interest groups involve them in the internal operations of these private groups? Does the scholar of public administration find useful data in the administration of large, private corporations? About these questions political scientists agree only that they involve the frontiers of the discipline and territories which other disciplines have claimed.

The political system, then, is what the political scientist studies; but the question of the nature of political science is also a question of the goals and purposes with which they approach political data. Are they to be detached scientists, building explanatory theories of politics? Or is their chief responsibility the clarification of society's political goals, the quest for the just and good life? Or are they to fuse the two into a policy science which can provide citizens and officeholders with strategies for reaching specified goals? On the answers to these questions American political scientists are, again, by no means agreed. The current status of their ferments, their indecisions, and their disagreements forms a focus for the following chapter.

The Growth
and Development
of Political Science
in America

chapter two

Rare indeed is the political scientist who has not faced the question, "Is political science *really* a science?" Sometimes the questioner is amused, sometimes skeptical. Often he is genuinely confused. Regardless of how the political scientist answers the question, the chances are that he rarely admits that the question is one that continues, on a somewhat more sophisticated level, to plague political scientists themselves. For the issue of whether political science can achieve the systematic, ordered, predictive propositions we associate with a "science" remains the most hotly debated issue within the profession itself.

The issue of a science of politics has been revived in the years since World War II by the advent of a movement within political science which has attempted to steer the discipline toward the development of rigorous theoretical propositions by the use of more careful techniques and methods. Because this movement sought to ally political science more closely with the other behavioral sciences—sociology, anthropology, and psychology, especially—it has been referred to as "behaviorism" or "behavioralism." In its debate over the new behaviorism, political science has for the first time become overtly and self-consciously concerned about the methods and techniques of the social sciences and about its own goals and priorities. In the process political scientists have gone into a veritable orgy of self-appraisal and stock-taking. Their books, journals, and meetings have increasingly dealt with the question of "Whither political science?" [1]

[1] For example, see: David Easton, *The Political System* (New York: Alfred A. Knopf, Inc., 1953); Vernon Van Dyke, *Political Science: A Philosophic Analysis* (Palo Alto, Calif.: Stanford University Press, 1960); Dwight Waldo, *Political Science in the United States of America* (New York: UNESCO, 1956); Charles S. Hyneman, *The Study of Politics* (Urbana: University of Illinois Press, 1959); Harold Lasswell, *The Future of Political Science* (New York: Atherton Press, 1963); and Bernard Crick, *The American Science of Politics* (Berkeley: University of California Press, 1959).

This ferment within contemporary political science has too frequently been viewed as a simple two-sided struggle between the new behaviorists and the earlier "traditionalists." That simplification does not, unhappily, suggest the diversity and richness of approach that was common in the political science now referred to as "traditional." Nor does it indicate that the new scientific empiricism of the behaviorists has old and honorable roots within American political science, and that it is itself hardly a monolithic movement. To see the complexity of the current agitation within American political science one must look at the main influential traditions of its past.

THE MAIN CURRENTS IN AMERICAN POLITICAL SCIENCE

Political science in the United States is hardly old enough to have a very complicated or impressive history. Although its famous first practitioner, Francis Lieber, came to this country before the Civil War and to a chair at Columbia University in 1858, the teaching of political science in American colleges and universities did not become common until the turn of the century. Indeed, it long failed to gain its academic independence in many colleges, remaining often the junior partner in departments of history and political science (never departments of political science and history) until the 1940's and 1950's. Despite that extended state of dependence, an argument can be made that political science came of age in the United States in 1903 with the founding of the American Political Science Association and its official journal, the *American Political Science Review*. In a very real sense an academic discipline begins when its practitioners see common interests that merit an organization.

In the brief history of American political science one can perceive the development of a number of scholarly traditions. Four main currents—legalism, activism, philosophy, and science—stand out; but before turning to them, we should clearly understand one point: in the skirmishes within political science there have been neither victors nor vanquished. As new approaches have appeared, they have been absorbed into the discipline without expelling or displacing any of the older traditions or approaches. Consequently, political science became an amalgam of different and often conflicting approaches to the study of politics. Depending on how one viewed it, it was either chaos and confusion or a healthy intellectual pluralism.

The tradition of *legalism* came to political science from the prevailing European traditions of the nineteenth century. American scholars trained in the German centers brought it back to this country with their German Ph.D.'s. An examination of treatises such as Theodore Woolsey's reveals the early influence of this approach.[2] The concern is with legal and constitutional frameworks, with formal legal institutions, with legal rights and powers. The American Congress and President are discussed only in terms of their constitutional powers and structure. By the same token, the study of comparative government began as a comparison of the constitutions of major governments. The legal tradition continues with considerable power even today in American political science in courses in constitutional law, administrative law, international law, and, to a lesser extent, in courses studying legal regulation in the areas of labor, business, natural resources, agriculture, and social welfare. It is, in other words, the tradition in political science which is closest to the study of law and the concerns of legal scholars.

Intermittently over its short history American political science has been greatly influenced by another tradition, that of *activism and reform*. It began when political scientists joined with the reform traditions of American Progressivism to bring their knowledge to bear on the governmental problems of the day. They cooperated in the founding and staffing of legislative reference bureaus and institutes of governmental research. Scarcely a state university today is without a bureau of governmental or public-affairs research of some sort. Additionally, political scientists were in the forefront of movements for civil-service reform, city-manager and commission government at the local level, the reforms of direct democracy (the initiative, referendum, and recall), the direct primary, and nonpartisanship in political affairs. More recently this activism has focused on national and international affairs. During the 1930's and 1940's political scientists flocked to Washington, and since then they have been deeply involved in world affairs—in supporting the emerging international organizations, in limiting armaments, in developing systems for reducing international tensions. At the local level their activism has currently been channeled into direct political participation. Political scientists and their students are now more than ever involved in partisan politics, running for public office or serving on the staffs of elected officials. Within the political science curriculum today these activist traditions are represented in the professional orientation of courses in public administration, in courses in politics and field obser-

---

[2] Theodore Woolsey, *Political Science, or the State Theoretically and Practically Considered*, 2 vols. (New York: Charles Scribner's Sons, 1879).

vation, and in the reformist outlook that touches many courses dealing with foreign and domestic policy alternatives.[3]

The third of these main currents in American political science—the *philosophical*—involves one of political science's semantic curiosities, the field of "political theory." Whereas *theory* in other disciplines refers to propositions of a systematic, causal nature, in political science *theory* has traditionally referred to the study of important values, ideas, and doctrines about politics. The political theorists, through the examination of the classics of political philosophy from Plato and Aristotle to the present, have sought to clarify the basic components of the good life and identify the political arrangements which would best promote and insure them. Most generally the study of the great political ideas and doctrines has proceeded historically and has been limited largely to the Western political tradition. Its study has pivoted around the great and influential political thinkers: Plato, Aquinas, Machiavelli, Hobbes, Locke, Rousseau, Hegel, Marx. This tradition continues in force in courses in political theory and in the continuing concern of the discipline for basic political values, goals, and ideologies. It is the approach within political science which is closest to the disciplines of the humanities—philosophy and history, for example.[4]

Finally, as its very name would suggest, political science has from the beginning contained elements of *science*. As early as 1887 Woodrow Wilson, whose fame as a political scientist would be secure had he never won the Presidency of the United States, described the actual operations of Congress, including the fragmented power system of the two houses.[5] His was a study that depended on the empirical observations of actual behavior and processes in Congress. Also, at the turn of the century A. Lawrence Lowell was studying the cohesion of political parties in the British House of Commons.[6] In fact, political science has never been without advocates who were convinced that

---

[3] For an example of the political scientist as activist-reformer, see the career and writings of Luther Gulick.

[4] For examples of the philosophic tradition in American political science see two typical recent works: Thomas L. Thorson, *The Logic of Democracy* (New York: Holt, Rinehart & Winston, Inc., 1962) and Robert C. Tucker, *Philosophy and Myth in Karl Marx* (New York: Cambridge University Press, 1961).

[5] Woodrow Wilson, *Congressional Government* (New York: Meridian Books, 1956).

[6] For an excellent summary of Lowell's work and for other matters in the development of American political science, see Crick's *The American Science of Politics.* Useful also is Anna Haddow, *Political Science in American Colleges and Universities* (New York: Appleton-Century & Appleton-Century-Crofts, 1939).

the empirical study of political events and behavior would yield verifiable propositions about the political system. Frequently that empiricism was concerned with little more than sheer description or very restricted, specific assertions. Often it was more interested in reports of actual events than in general propositions of wide applicability; but often, too, it was concerned with broader theoretical significance. Prophets such as Arthur Bentley and Charles Merriam called repeatedly for the development of concepts and methods which would promote a rigorous, systematic science of politics.[7] Bentley's plea came in 1908, and Merriam's was made less than a generation later, in 1925—both well in advance of the behavioral movement.

Although it would be a colossal mistake to say that these four traditions comprise the totality of the "traditional" political science, they unquestionably dominated American political science at the advent of the second world war. Despite their different approaches to political phenomena, these traditions had some directions in common. They were all chiefly concerned with political and governmental institutions—with legislatures, executives, and courts; with political parties and elections; with international organizations and tribunals, with constitutions, public law, and international law. Conversely, they devoted little attention to behavioral decisions and processes within the institutions—to the political behavior of individuals or to the role behavior of officeholders, for example. Secondly, they shared a common disposition to historicism and chronology as a way of organizing their materials. Most of the textbooks in American government even today begin with the founding fathers and the writing of the American constitution. Lacking a systematic body of data, political scientists drew on historical examples; and lacking a body of theory and concepts, they sought the sequential, developmental analysis of history. Finally, these traditions shared a distrust of generalizations and the probing for systematic explanation. Political scientists considered themselves practical men of action with a mission in the real world. They shared a confidence, which in hindsight seems more than a little naive, that readily observed facts would speak for themselves. The layman's view of the world, they thought, needed no special form of political analysis.

On the eve of World War II, then, American political science was something of a special case in the social sciences. It had no cen-

---

[7] See, for example, Arthur Bentley, *The Process of Government* (Chicago: University of Chicago Press, 1908) and Charles Merriam, *New Aspects of Politics* (Chicago: University of Chicago Press, 1925).

tral, organizing set of concepts or body of theory, as did the discipline of economics. It shared little of the interest of anthropology, sociology, and psychology for understanding the individual, his socialization, his motivation, and his behavior. It did share the confidence of history in the unadorned fact, the "objective" narrative, and the organizing and analytical value of "time." Yet its concern with philosophical questions, with central values and the good life, and with active participation in public affairs took it away from the historian's ivory tower and greater commitment to objectivity. It shared some concerns with philosophy, the humanities, and the law, and some, too, with the vocationally oriented public-service professions. It was a heterogeneous, plural, and diverse discipline with little agreement about its central concerns, its methods, and its basic goals. It was a discipline uncomfortable in building theoretical propositions and perfecting methodologies. Above all, it was a discipline without a clear intellectual identity.

POLITICAL SCIENCE AS BEHAVIORAL SCIENCE

These were the traditions that the postwar behaviorists challenged; but their advocacy of a more rigorous empiricism and a theory of politics was, as we have seen, hardly new to political science. By the 1920's and 1930's a group of political scientists, centered at the University of Chicago, had crystallized this scientific spirit into something of a school or movement. It centered around Charles Merriam, a founder and the first president of the Social Science Research Council and author of the call to scientific arms, *New Aspects of Politics.* Drawing on the concepts and techniques already in use in sociology and psychology, Merriam and his students brought to political science fresh insights, current statistical techniques of description and analysis, and a new concern with individual and ·small-group behavior. In the decades that followed, the work of the Merriam movement was carried on by Harold Lasswell, still a creative innovator in American political science today.[8]

In fact, it is probably no exaggeration to say that the "new" political science of the behaviorists is a logical and direct extension

---

[8] Lasswell's work is illustrated and typified by: *Politics: Who Gets What, When, How* (New York: McGraw-Hill Book Co., Inc., 1936); *Power and Personality* (New York: W. W. Norton & Company, Inc., 1948); and, with Abraham Kaplan, *Power and Society* (New Haven, Conn.: Yale University Press, 1950).

of the Chicago movement of twenty years before. Had not the war intervened and disrupted the natural development of the profession, that tie would be more apparent. The wartime contributions of the other behavioral sciences, the new prestige of science itself, the financial prodding of the foundations, and a dissatisfaction with the fruits of the earlier political science augmented and intensified the prewar movement. Causes aside, however, it has become the single most influential movement in postwar political science and the stimulus and focus of an assessment within the discipline of its goals and methods.

Although the behavioral movement might, for want of unity and explicit goals, be better called a mood or spirit, most behaviorists are agreed that they want political science to adopt, in varying degrees:

1. *New data.* They would bring to the study of politics a new concern for the individual and group behavior that goes on within political institutions. They would, for instance, study the role of political leadership and elites and the influence of a congressman's role-perception on the way he carries out his responsibilities. In other words, they have sought to draw political science away from its almost exclusive concern with formal institutions and toward the political actors and processes.

2. *New methods.* The behaviorists have propounded a more rigorous and systematic empiricism, one that observes more closely, records more precisely, and uses more sophisticated concepts and tools of analysis than political science has in the past. Tables, graphs, scales, charts, and mathematical models have become their trademarks; field work has virtually become their way of life.

3. *New concepts.* The new political science has drawn freely on the analytical vocabulary of the other behavioral sciences for new categories and concepts. Some, of course, they have developed for themselves. In either event, however, the goal is a technical vocabulary which will identify the more abstract, analytical relationships necessary for the development of theoretical generalizations. As a result, political scientists show a new ease with terms such as *power, elite,* and *role,* not to mention *functional prerequisites* and *political socialization.*

4. *New theoretical goals.* Above all, the new mood in political science seeks to impel the discipline toward generalizations which will explain relationships within the political system. It is the old goal, more cautiously presented, of a science of politics. The behaviorists have brought the hypothesis and theoretical proposition back into

even narrowly circumscribed research. At the same time they continue the search for the towering, over-all theoretical edifice which will integrate and unify the more specific findings and propositions of the discipline.[9]

Unhappily, there has been some tendency within even the knowledgeable precincts of political science to view the challenge of the behaviorists in elemental, black-white terms. In reality, however, the agitation and ferment within contemporary political science hardly pits all "traditionalists" against all "behaviorists" in a winner-take-all battle for the life and soul of the discipline. The battle lines, if the image may be used, are not that clear, straight, and rigid. Consider just these points:

1. All of the goals of the new political science have had supporters and practitioners within political science for over half a century. One can even cite that early political scientist, Aristotle, who some 2,300 years ago set down theoretical propositions about relationships between socio-economic status and political power.[10] The issue, then, is not striking innovations, but greater emphasis on earlier commitments.

2. The new political science is scarcely a monolithic movement with a universally accepted creed. Its adherents may and do differ over priorities in formulating theory—over whether to build the system from the bottom with narrow-gauge propositions or whether first to aim for the single, over-arching theory. They differ, too, over the usefulness of various methods, concepts, and analytical techniques. Their differences extend to specifics—to the value, for instance, of a particular statistical measure of judicial voting behavior.

3. The confrontation of the new and the old political science has hardly produced an either-or choice. Many political scientists trained in and familiar with the older traditions have accepted in varying degrees the worth of behaviorism. For their part, very few of the behaviorists would discard the established traditions. In fact, it seems clear that the confrontation will be resolved as have all similar ones in the past: not by total victory, but by the absorption of the new into the old. If the result is not an integrated synthesis, it will at least be a more vital mixture.

---

[9] For stimulating essays on the behavioral movement see: Heinz Eulau, *The Behavioral Persuasion in Politics* (New York: Random House, Inc., 1963); Austin Ranney (ed.), *Essays on the Behavioral Study of Politics* (Urbana: University of Illinois Press, 1962); and Robert Dahl, "The Behavioral Approach," *American Political Science Review*, LV (December, 1961), 763–72.

[10] *The Politics*, Book IV.

Even with all these qualifications, something of a battle *does* rage over the new political science. The chief attack on it has come from those within the discipline who doubt the ability of empirical methods to discover enough about political men and institutions to develop theoretical propositions. They point to the almost infinite complexity of human behavior and to the special difficulties of knowing human attitudes and motivation. They argue the inability of the scholar to subject political phenomena to controlled experiments in the way he might if his actors were rats or primates. They note, too, that humans know when they are being studied and may adjust their behavior as a result; the voter questioned repeatedly during a campaign may increase his political awareness, and this may affect his vote. Above all, they argue that the scholar cannot achieve the same objectivity and detachment when his concern is political behavior as he may when it is the behavior of fruit flies or an isotope of carbon. The critics of behaviorism have, in other words, restated the full canon of arguments against the transfer of science and the scientific methods to the study of human behavior.

A second body of criticism grows out of the first. It is that the new political scientists, in chasing their theoretical will-o'-the-wisp, squander time and resources that could more profitably be spent in the examination of pressing public questions. While they pursue their inconsequential laboring of the obvious and the trivial, the charge goes, who is to examine the nature of justice and equality, the confrontation of the nuclear powers, the dangers of the population explosion, the clash of powerful ideologies? The charge is essentially one of ivory-towerism—that the new political scientists pursue their scientific truths while the problems of modern man go unexamined.[11]

The contemporary debate in American political science, then, is over fundamentals. It concerns, first of all, the very epistomology, the very theory of knowledge, underlying research in political science. Secondly, it touches the priorities of the discipline—with what kinds of tasks should political scientists be occupied? It is, indeed, the first wide-ranging debate over methods and goals which the discipline has seen.

---

[11] Recent trenchant, and often severe, criticism of the new political science can be found in: Leo Strauss, *What Is Political Philosophy?* (New York: Free Press of Glencoe, Inc., 1959); Herbert Storing (ed.), *Essays on the Scientific Study of Politics* (New York: Holt, Rinehart & Winston, Inc., 1962); and James Charlesworth (ed.), *The Limits of Behavioralism in Political Science* (Philadelphia: American Academy of Political and Social Science, 1962).

WHITHER AMERICAN POLITICAL SCIENCE?

An assessment of the future of American political science begins, of necessity, with an assessment of its present. Although one might need the perspective of time to judge the impact of the new behaviorism on the whole of the discipline, it seems clear for the moment that its impact has been substantial. One look at the journals of political science in the United States [12] or at the programs of the profession's annual national and regional conventions confirms the advance of behaviorism. Each of the fields of contemporary political science has felt its impact. The field of constitutional law, long one of the bastions of legalism and institutionalism, increasingly welcomes a body of literature on the politics of litigation, on interest-group activity in managing test cases, on the behavior of judges and courts, and on the impact of judicial action on other branches of government and the public at large. The field of comparative government, long little more than the description and evaluation of major foreign governments, has expanded to a genuine comparison and theoretical analysis of political institutions and processes.

Perhaps most significant for the future, the new political science has had its greatest success and vogue at the large educational centers which offer most of the American graduate training in political science. As their young graduates fan out into the teaching profession they will, in various ways, carry the new political science with them.

However, even though the behaviorists have become the major new voice in the political science profession, some of their colleagues have recently spoken out on behalf of other goals and priorities within the discipline. Two of them, Leo Strauss and Harold Lasswell, deserve more than passing mention. Their stature in the discipline would entitle them to a hearing; but, in addition, they reflect the gnawing doubts of other political scientists.

---

[12] The journals dealing with the full range of political science in the United States are really four: the *American Political Science Review, Journal of Politics, Midwest Journal of Political Science*, and *Western Political Quarterly*. They are published by the American Political Science Association, the Southern Political Science Association, the Midwest Conference of Political Scientists, and the Western Political Science Association, respectively. *The Review of Politics*, published at Notre Dame University, might also be included, although the range of its intellectual interests is narrower than those of the four journals named above. Despite its name *The Political Science Quarterly* is really a journal of the social sciences and history.

Strauss and a group of his former students have mounted the most wide-ranging attack on the new political science. He has denounced in the severest strictures both its pretentions to scientific knowledge of behavior and its moral relativism. The Straussians would repair instead to common-sense, intuitive knowledge of the political world. Necessary political knowledge, they argue, can be perceived by the intelligent, broadly educated, rational man. The goal of their political science would be an understanding of those political arrangements which can best promote basic human values and the development of human potential of the individual. Theirs is the classic Greek goal of political science as the queen of the liberal disciplines, the one leading to the knowledge and the achievement of the good society. It is a vision of political scientists as philosophers and generalists rather than scientists and specialists.[13]

One of the discipline's most creative scholars, Harold Lasswell, has also addressed himself recently to a statement of the goals for political science in the coming decades.[14] Lasswell, unlike the Straussians, accepts the behaviorists' empirical methods and their desire to develop a theory of politics; but he turns additionally to the question of "Knowledge for what?" and proposes that political science mobilize its verifiable propositions to help solve the public's pressing problems. Political science, in his vision, would be the "policy science"—both science and reform movement. He proposes centers of advanced political science in which political scientists would combine their knowledge of the political processes with the specialized knowledge of other scholars—economists, geneticists, and nuclear engineers, for instance— to propose solutions to contemporary problems, whether they be the endemic poverty of the developing nations or the threat of nuclear holocaust. For Lasswell political science must be at the same time a science of politics, a philosophic examination of the ends and goals of man, and a practical profession engaged in advising electorates and men of power.

Contemporary political science, then, is still looking for an identity; but this search, self-conscious though it may appear at times, has not been bought at the price of conformity and a new orthodoxy. The older, more traditional modes remain. *Eclecticism* and *diversity* remain the watchwords. The questions which political science is asking, furthermore, are the most basic ones, the ones which define the

---

[13] See Strauss, *What Is Political Philosophy?* and Storing, *Essays on the Scientific Study of Politics.*

[14] *The Future of Political Science.*

goals and direction of a discipline and which provide a yardstick to its development: the questions of its boundaries, its system of knowledge, and its goals.

Boundaries

As was indicated in the last chapter, political science has devoted enormous energy in the past generation to defining what it means by *the political* and what, therefore, it will study. Its boundaries have expanded to include the political behavior of individuals and small groups—voting behavior, political socialization, leadership and elites, for instance. It has as well become concerned with the interaction of individuals and groups within the institutions of government. It has engaged in interdisciplinary work—such as work in the theory of organizations—and it has tried to relate the theoretical concerns and concepts of political science to the other social sciences.

System of Knowledge

Political science was empirical at heart even when it scarcely thought about epistemological matters. Its implicit faith has been in knowledge by sense observation of events in the real world. Its empiricism is now, however, more sophisticated, more rigorous, more precise. The old confidence in the uninterpreted "fact" is gone. In its place is a greater awareness of the power of theory and hypothesis in the discovery of reality, a greater awareness of the necessity to organize the "facts" into meaningful relationships.

The Goals

It is here that the major battle over priorities within political science takes place. Is political science to press for the development of a theory or theories of politics? Or is it to pursue the clarification of individual values and social objectives? Both goals remain within the traditions of the profession. A third goal of activism and reform also remains; but it, too, has been transformed. There is probably an increasing awareness within political science that successful activism must rest at bottom on a broader range of verified knowledge about the political system than it has in the past. It now appears that some of the profession's early enthusiasms—for example, the one for nonpartisanship in state and local government—may have resulted from an imperfect understanding of the political processes. Would-be activists in the profession also recognize that realization of their political objectives may be hastened by their entrance into political arenas.

Their activism, in other words, has been quickened by the fear that no one is listening and by the conviction that in a democracy perhaps no one ought to listen to experts simply because they are experts.

The safest conclusion to make about the history of American political science over the years since World War II seems to be that it has been an age of discovery for the discipline. Questioning, introspection, self-evaluation, and the quest for identity have followed the loss of innocence. Gone is the unexamined, comforting faith in the scholarly status quo. For the moment the discipline appears to be finding its identity in a closer relation with the data, the methods, and the goals of the behavioral sciences. But so long as the examination continues, no approach is immune from question.

The Tools
of the chapter three
Political Scientist

Political science is an inveterate borrower. It may, in fact, be the great eclectic among the social sciences. The history of its growth and development is a history of selecting skills and ideas from the other social sciences, of integrating the new with the old, of reinvigorating old traditions with new borrowings and adaptations. Most recently, as we have seen, political science has drawn heavily on the concepts, the techniques, and the theories of sociology, anthropology, and psychology.

Inevitably, therefore, political scientists bring different methods, techniques, and skills to their scholarly work. There are, for example, political scientists who question samples of voters about their Presidential preferences, those who observe United Nations agencies in operation, those who translate and interpret the political writings of Marsiglio of Padua, and those who analyze the printed opinions and decisions of judicial bodies. The specific skills they need and use may range from the ability to understand the legalisms of a court to the ability to program factor analysis on a computer.

Regardless of their different skills and methods, political scientists do share some basic commitments to scholarly methods. Although they "practice" it in many ways, they are committed by and large to the basic tenets of empiricism. That is to say, they are in varying ways committed to the proposition that knowledge of social behavior and institutions must come from experience, from sense perception of events in the real world. Knowledge for the empiricist is a series of generalizations based on observations of specific instances and events. Political scientists may differ in how systematically they think these observations must be made and recorded, but the basic commitment to empiricism is there nonetheless.

Perhaps the commitment to empiricism might be put another way. Political scientists agree fundamentally about what the "facts" are in the world of events and about how one proceeds to make generalizations from them. They share a definition of *evidence* as that which can be observed, and they hesitate to accept a "fact" without sufficient weight of evidence. Consequently, they seek original reports and documents, or they observe behavior or question other observers. Furthermore, they share the scientist's rigorous methods of testing hypotheses and propositions with empirical evidence. They do not, in other words, rely on contemplation or excogitation as ways of learning about politics. Nor do they deduce explanation of specific events or actions from general principles about what seems "natural," or "reasonable," or "logical."

Even though there are exceptions to these generalizations, the main path within political science remains that of empiricism, and a discussion of the methods of the political scientist may reasonably focus on those of the empirical tradition. The analysis which follows will touch three aspects of the scholarly task: the methods political scientists use to acquire and describe data, the techniques they have for analyzing it, and the ways in which they attack a scholarly problem.

GETTING THE DATA

The methods and techniques the political scientist uses in acquiring his data depend on the nature of the data he seeks. A study concerned with the international system of the nineteenth century or the role of the American Cabinet in wartime would have to depend largely on the documents, newspaper reports, personal accounts, correspondence, diaries, memoirs, and official state papers that the historian customarily examines. A study of the political socialization of American children betwen the ages of six and ten is quite another matter. Only observation, interviewing, and written questionnaires will yield the necessary data. The data one sets out to discover, then, in part determine the scholarly methods one uses. And since the data a discipline seeks are largely set by the goals and self-image of the discipline, we come back again to the ferment in political science over goals and trends. In the broadest terms, the particular patterns of skills a political scientist possesses depend to a great extent on his views of the discipline and of the job of the political scientist.

One of the chief manifestations of the new political science has been its desire to explore new problems. It has tried to learn more about behavior and processes about which little recorded or published data exist—more about leadership relationships, about patterns of power and influence, about political attitudes and preferences, about the informal decision-making processes. Much of its criticism of the more traditional political science, indeed, has centered on the traditional preoccupation with political institutions and the formal, documentary record of their operations. Earlier political science appeared far more committed to the kinds of data the historian used than those used by other social scientists. It appeared, in short, often tied to the library desk. To expand their data-collecting the new political scientists have had to go into the field with the other behavioral disciplines.

Perhaps an illustration will clarify this expansion of data and the skills necessary to acquire them. In the 1930's and 1940's most of the studies of American voting behavior depended on the analysis of published vote totals and census data. The scholar would relate variations in election data for wards, cities, or counties to variations in other characteristics of their populations—their religious composition, educational level, or per capita income. With such data the scholar might find that low-income districts voted for Democratic candidates or that Protestant counties favored Republicans. Such analysis had its limitations, however. It failed to answer questions about how individuals made their decisions or why they made the ones they did. It also dealt with large aggregates, and it could establish relationships only for large groups of voters. Precision of analysis was virtually impossible.

In the last twenty years scholars have turned to surveys of voter samples, in which individuals are interviewed several times during a campaign and once after it. The interviewing determines not only their specific social characteristics but their political attitudes and outlooks, their party preferences, their candidate preferences, the sources of their political information, and the process by which they make political decisions. The acquisition of this kind of voting data has been possible only because social scientists have developed new skills in sampling a population of voters (one of the most reputable scholarly surveys of the entire American electorate uses a sample of fewer than 2,000), in constructing and asking questions, and in analyzing and tabulating the responses. So, with new scholarly tools

American political scientists have begun to answer some puzzling questions about the American voter.[1]

Even with the advent of behaviorism, however, the traditional materials and skills of the library remain indispensable for the political scientist. He is highly dependent on the verbatim reports of legislative debates, on records of committee action, roll-call votes, and the laws passed by legislatures. He uses the papers, messages, and statements of Presidents and administrative officers—whether they be the formal prose of the State of the Union message or the off-hand comment of the press conference. He needs the reports, records, and documents of the United Nations and its subsidiary agencies, as well as vote totals, census data, and official documents for all major governments. For many of his studies—of the power of the British Prime Minister in the Cabinet or the making of the Presidential decision to support an invaded ally, for example—he may rely on less formal sources: memoirs, diaries, letters, personal papers, memoranda, and newspaper accounts. The scholars of the development of political ideas may go back to the manuscripts of great thinkers of the past, armed with the skills of the translator and the calligrapher.

For those political scientists familiar with computers and field interviewing, scholarly work in the library may seem a little tame and old fashioned. Yet mastery of the library's range of bibliographic tools is no simple task. Although it is true that political scientists do not differ greatly from other scholars in the way they use the library, there is a set of bibliographic tools which are especially useful in their work. Probably few other disciplines find the fully indexed issues of the *New York Times* as useful as political science does; nor would many other disciplines be so reliant on the periodical and book listings, by subject matter, of the annual volumes of the Public Affairs Information Service. Certainly no other discipline can so profit from a mastery of the obscure labyrinths of the United States government document file; so great are the skills needed here, in fact, that most political scientists simply throw themselves on the mercies of a good documents librarian, if their library is fortunate enough to have one.

Mastery of the library and its aids not only makes inquiry possible; it may even add some of the excitement of the chase. The

---

[1] The older analysis of aggregate vote totals is typified by Arthur N. Holcombe's *New Party Politics* (New York: W. W. Norton & Company, Inc., 1933). For examples of the newer studies based on sample survey data, see Bernard Berelson *et al.*, *Voting* (Chicago: University of Chicago Press, 1954) and Angus Campbell *et al.*, *The American Voter* (New York: John Wiley & Sons, Inc., 1960).

secret, of course, is to know what data the library contains and how they can most easily be exploited. The man who knows the tools will have no difficulty in finding the cases in which the Supreme Court has interpreted the Taft-Hartley Labor Management Relations Act of 1947. He who doesn't know them will never find out, largely because he does not know it is possible to find out. The crucial skill with libraries, as with computers, is to know "what can be done" with them. It is only secondarily important to be able to do it oneself.

The library assumes a great role even for the political scientists who get most or all of their data from the field. It is in the library that they must search the literature of the discipline—where they must find what others have found before them. The individual scholar cannot discover everything anew for himself, and even in the areas of his own research, he must be able to build on the work of others if political science is to be a cumulating body of comparable knowledge about politics. There is another kind of scholarly contribution within political science which depends on the works of other scholars: the integrative, theoretical works. These are works which bring the findings of others together, generalize about them, give them order and meaning. David Truman, for example, in *The Governmental Process*,[2] drew on the writings of many scholars about American politics, put them into the framework of a group theory of politics, and produced a systematic and perceptive analysis of the American political system. Truman's contribution was to provide the organizing and explanatory frame of reference.

For all his dependence on the library and traditional methods, today's political scientist is increasingly going into the field. He may interview participants in or close observers of the political system, drawing on their firsthand knowledge; he may, for instance, question officials in a farm organization about how they decide on political goals and tactics. Or he may combine that interviewing with his own direct observation; in studying a political party he may attend its meetings, caucuses, and conventions, observe its campaigns, watch its fund-raising tribulations. Or he may become an actual participant in the groups and processes he wants to study; he may work as a party official, run for a local council, or work as an administrative assistant to a governor or a congressman. His field work may, moreover, cover more than one of these forms, and it may also be combined with the more traditional library researches.

---

2 New York: Alfred A. Knopf, Inc., 1951.

If the subject of study, however, is the individual political man or political men in small groups, more systematic field research may be called for. When one interviews individuals for data about themselves rather than others—that is, when one treats them as subjects rather than informants—he must either interview the full universe (for example, all the American voters, or all members of a specific union) or a representative sample of it. Then with careful questions the political scientist may discover the respondent's background and social characteristics, his political values, his attitudes on public issues, and the decisions he thinks he would make in certain circumstances. These sample survey methods have most frequently been used to probe the political consciousness of voters; but they can be used as well to test the political awareness of children, the feelings of nationalism among peoples of developing areas, or the ways in which administrative officials perceive their jobs and their responsibilities to them.

Political scientists continue to sharpen their methods in other ways. They have, for example, increasingly tried to describe the data more precisely. Often that means merely saying "82.3 per cent of the time" rather than "generally" or "most of the time." Frequently, however, it means the construction of complicated scales and indexes. Secondly, they have tried to refine the categories and concepts—the "measuring units"—by which they acquire data. Political scientists have tried to refine concepts such as *power* so that they can be measured—the problem is one of determining A's power over B in a specific situation. Finally, in advancing their data collection some political scientists have pushed into new realms in search of useful data. Some have begun controlled experiments—studying, for example, the democratic processes of reaching consensus by a small group in a structured situation created and observed by the scholar. Other scholars have begun to employ "simulation"—the re-creation of real decision-making situations. Students or adults may act the roles of nations in the international system, for instance, with the expectation that their reactions and decisions in the simulated situations will offer insight into the behavior of nations and the men who guide their international destinies.[3]

Other problems in collecting data remain largely on tomorrow's agenda. The printed page and the library have traditionally been the repository of scholarly data and knowledge. In the library the storing,

---

[3] The possibilities of simulation in the social sciences are explored by Harold Guetzkow *et al.*, *Simulation in International Relations: Developments for Research and Teaching* (Englewood Cliffs, N.J.: Prentice-Hall, Inc., 1963).

exchange, and easy availability of basic data is assured. Increasingly, however, the data of the discipline are not systematically reported, published, or stored. One scholar may have data on the backgrounds of legislators in his state, and another may possess data on interviews with Indonesian labor leaders. But how does one make these data available to other scholars? In an attempt to solve this problem, the Survey Research Center of the University of Michigan has set up an interuniversity clearing house, not only for its own survey data on the American electorate, but for that of other studies and data as well. It is now possible for a scholar at one of the member schools to write the Center and receive on IBM cards the major data of a study conducted five years before by scholars 2,000 miles away.

Political science, then, encompasses a vast range of skills and methods in collecting its data—broad enough to embrace the range of its concerns from the political attitudes of retired workers to the strategies behind the use of nuclear deterrents. And scholars increasingly realize the difficulties in collecting them. Often data are complex —as complex as the rationale of an intelligent political leader. Often they are elusive or unavailable—as unavailable as the debates of the justices of the Supreme Court. Often they cannot be controlled or repeated—as one does not restage a British general election to hold some factor constant; and often the data are bound up with the enthusiasms and feelings of the scholar, for political scientists are men aware of their times and society and sensitive to them.

ANALYSIS OF THE DATA

Analysis follows the collection of data. If his investigations are well planned, the political scientist has formulated the kinds of questions he will ask, the kinds of relationships he is attempting to demonstrate. He doesn't just fiddle aimlessly with the data to see what will turn up, although it is certainly true that every scholar has in the course of his work seen unexpected relationships emerge.

Basically, the goal of political science is the development of generalizations and theories about political behavior and political systems. Since it has only recently begun to develop its knowledge of the political, political science is still building its descriptive generalizations. Its practitioners know little of the operation of the political systems of Africa or Asia or South America. There are even great lacunae in knowledge about the American governments; there is little in the literature, for example, about the operation and role of the American courts other than the Supreme Court. The task at this descriptive level is the answering of the "how" questions, the identification of the ways and processes through which political systems function.

From this attempt at descriptive generalization it is only a short step to show relationships—to shift from the "how" to the "why" questions. As soon as descriptive generalizations begin to disclose variations, we look for variations in other factors related to those at hand. Political scientists see cabinet instability in some parliamentary systems, such as those of the Third and Fourth Republics in France; in others they see impressive stability—in Britain no Cabinet has fallen in a vote of no confidence for almost seventy years. The difference begs for explanation. Political scientists have noted parallel variation in party systems, a multi-party system in France and a two-party system in Britain. The concomitant variations suggest a relationship, and the plausibility of the relationship is enhanced because political scientists can see the causal mechanism—the precise ways in which a multi-party system leads to unstable cabinet coalitions; and in seeing that relationship they push the analysis from the "how's" of cabinet government to the "why's" of it.

In reaching for these theories and generalizations the political scientist depends ultimately, as do all social scientists, on something very close to intuition or "insight." He observes a number of events or actions, and he finds relationships and commonalities in them. He must deduce general principles or fundamental relationships from his observations of specific and particular events. The skills he uses to perceive these wholes, patterns, and relationships are not easy to define; but they come close to the nub of creativity. It is not a thought process, however, which takes place in an intellectual vacuum. Earlier knowledge and researches provide clues to possible relationships. The insight, the perception of relationship, into the causes of cabinet instability flows easily and logically from knowledge both of cabinet government and of political parties.

Increasingly, since its behavioral trend began, American political science has been interested in perceiving and expressing these relationships more precisely. Relationship, for instance, may be expressed simply in a table of percentages:

Wards Carried by:	Wards of an American City	
	High Income Wards	Low Income Wards
Democrats	15%	78%
Republicans	85%	22%

The relationship between income levels and party voting is clear in the table above; just as clearly it would not exist if the figures were between 45 per cent and 55 per cent in all four parts of the table. More precise measures of relationship than the percentage table are available, however. The coefficient of correlation permits one to relate the variation in one set of data (to take the same illustration, the per capita income of the wards) with variation in another set (the percentage of the two-party vote won by the parties). It has a number of advantages over the percentage table. It can measure more subtle variations, and it can use precise data rather than the broad categories necessary in the table. Also, the relationship can be expressed more precisely on a continuum from $+1.0$ (perfect positive correlation) through 0 (no correlation) to -1.0 (perfect inverse correlation). Beyond this measure of correlation, the political scientist may begin to measure variation involving more than one variable through multiple-correlation techniques of various kinds.[4]

Another new technique of analysis, attitude-scaling, has recently found its way into political science. Developed during World War II by social psychologists, it proved useful to political scientists during the 1950's and 1960's. As a technique it is an attempt to arrange the attitudes of individuals by their intensity. Perhaps an illustration will help. Basically, scaling proceeds on the assumption that men aware of the public context and consequences of attitudes will respond in predictable patterns in response to specific statements on a single subject. To take an illustration about attitudes toward organized labor, one would expect these predictable patterns of responses:

---

[4] Political scientists find useful the little book by V. O. Key on standard statistical measures, A Primer of Statistics for Political Scientists (New York: The Crowell-Collier Publishing Co., 1954). A fuller excellent treatment of the techniques of social statistical analysis may be found in Hubert Blalock, Social Statistics (New York: McGraw-Hill Book Co., 1960).

	Pattern 1	Pattern 2	Pattern 3	Pattern 4
1. All trade unions ought to be outlawed.	Yes	No	No	No
2. Trade unions of government workers ought to be outlawed.	Yes	Yes	No	No
3. Some kinds of strikes ought to be outlawed.	Yes	Yes	Yes	No

One would not, in other words, expect someone to agree with the first statement and not with the others; one would not expect yes-no-no, yes-no-yes, or no-yes-no response patterns. If the attitude statements can be so ordered (as they are above in the 1, 2, 3 order) to provide the same staggered pattern of responses as one sees above, they are "scalable." That is to say, they can be arranged in the order of the intensity of responses to them.

Political scientists have applied this technique of analysis to the votes and decisions of legislators and judges, as well as to the attitudes of voters and citizens. To apply it to legislators, one must assume that their votes for or against legislation are "yes" and "no" responses to attitudinal statements. To carry the above illustration forward, one finds before the Congress bills—or amendments to bills— that touch labor issues; he then ranks the votes of congressmen on a number of these legislative proposals. In order to achieve the ordered pattern of the scale—assuming, of course, that the items *can* be scaled—the order of the items of both axes have to be juggled and rearranged. The final achievement of a scale tells the political scientist a number of things.

Congressmen Voting on Bills							
Bills	Smith	Jones	Black	White	Green	Gray	Miller
No. 2	yes	yes	no	no	no	no	no
No. 6	yes	yes	yes	no	no	no	no
No. 1	yes	yes	yes	no	no	no	no
No. 4	yes	yes	yes	yes	no	no	no
No. 8	yes	yes	yes	yes	no	no	no
No. 5	yes	yes	yes	yes	yes	no	no
No. 3	yes	yes	yes	yes	yes	yes	yes
No. 7	yes	yes	yes	yes	yes	yes	yes

It ranks the attitudes (the bills) from those with which there is the greatest agreement to those with which there is greatest disagreement. It also ranks the congressmen according to their relative position on this scale of attitudes; that ranking may also help identify blocs of congressmen with similar attitudes on the question. Since a perfect scale is rare, it will identify those congressmen whose votes do not fit the scale pattern; the scholar may then explore the reasons for their attitudinally inconsistent voting. Finally, the information of the scale may be used in additional analysis. For example, one might relate the different positions of congressmen on such a scale to their differences in party, in the vote margins by which they are elected, or in the social compositions of their districts.[5]

There are, of course, many other analytical methods and techniques available to the imaginative political scientist. Some deal with empirical data; but because of the philosophic tradition within the discipline, others do not. Some forms of philosophic analysis would, for example, subject the thought of a man or movement to the most punishing, rigorous tests of its logic and internal consistency. Studies in other traditions would examine the basic truth of ethical and value statements by rational inquiry into the "natural" and right principles that inhere in the nature of rational man and a rightly ordered society. Others would instead examine the meanings and uses of language. Still others question the efficacy of means to desired ends or the practical consequences of the pursuit of goal A rather than goal B.

Political science remains, however, largely concerned with the finding of relationships in empirical data. Beyond the discovery of these relationships it is directed to the problem of cause and effect. Political scientists, like most other social scientists, are skittish about moving into the complex territory of social causation. Their vocabularies are filled with words which hedge the matter of cause; terms such as *factors, determinants, influences,* and *forces* all suggest cause while dodging responsibility for identifying it. Yet the scholar knows that persisting relationships are not necessarily causal in nature. One can show a relationship in the American electorate between graduating from college and voting Republican, but it is unlikely that the college experience itself causes large numbers to vote Republican. Probably the explanation lies in the relatively high socio-economic status of both the well-educated and the Republicans. Indeed, the relationship

---

5 The use of scale analysis in recent American political science is amply illustrated by Duncan MacRae, *Dimensions of Congressional Voting* (Berkeley: University of California Press, 1958) and Glendon Schubert, *Quantitative Analysis of Judicial Behavior* (New York: Free Press of Glencoe, Inc., 1959).

between any two variables may be explained in one of three ways: the relationship may be a chance one; one may cause the other in whole or in part; or outside causes may produce the relationship between the two. Frequently the most difficult job of the scholar is to determine which is the proper explanation.

Although most of the analysis of the social sciences is at least implicitly directed to cause, another form of analysis has recently become popular. It is functional analysis, another importation from the scholarship of sociology. Functionalism assumes the unity of the political system as an on-going set of institutions and processes which contribute to the well-being, the functioning, of the system. If the components, specific political institutions and processes, disturb that on-going operation of the system, they are "dysfunctional." The questions one asks in functional analysis, therefore, are ones of function rather than of cause. What does a particular part of the system contribute to the well-being of the whole? Granted that the British House of Lords does not do what it did 100 years ago, what is its present function in the British political system? Do political parties perform the same functions in one-party, two-party, and multi-party systems? If there is only a single viable political party, do other agencies or institutions perform the function of expressing dissent and raising policy alternatives? Basically, the tool of functional analysis allows the scholar to move either from the function to identify the agency which performs it, or from the agency to identify the function or functions which it performs.[6]

THE STRATEGIES OF RESEARCH

Behind every piece of scholarly research stands a strategy of attack, a master plan which states the problem and outlines the ways of marshalling evidence. The plan or design first of all defines the range and scope of the study; it stakes out a workable scholarly plot in the vast political fields. It also locates some part of the political system which will conveniently yield the kind of data the scholar needs. For the political scientist, like the astronomer, must of necessity take his data as it is available in the real world. He cannot create it experimentally.

---

[6] A recent, influential book employing functional analysis, especially in its introductory analytical framework, is Gabriel Almond and James S. Coleman, *The Politics of the Developing Areas* (Princeton, N.J.: Princeton University Press, 1960).

In setting their research strategies, political scientists have developed some categories or kinds of attacks on their scholarly problems. Four they mention most frequently are those which they call historical, comparative, co-variate, and case studies. Unfortunately, there is little consensus among political scientists on the precise meaning of those categories; but despite imprecisions of meaning, despite the fact that these are overlapping categories, and despite the fact that there are other strategies of approach current in political science, they do illustrate the approximate kinds of research designs political scientists use. It is useful and illustrative to examine them, provided that one keeps these cautions clearly in mind.

Historical Studies

Most political scientists, when they refer to the historical method mean more than the study of the past or the use of noncontemporary data. They refer to studies over a time span and organized by time sequences. By historical studies, therefore, we mean those which organize data, description, or analysis by chronology.

Historical studies have traditionally found their greatest value within political science in those areas most concerned with development over time. Much of the study of Western political thought has used the historical framework—a preference reflecting assumptions that great ideas evolve into others, that they draw on the intellectual past, that they reflect changes in society, and that the history of political ideas is marked by linkages and continuities over time. Hence, the scholars of ideas point to the influence of Locke on the American founding fathers, to the development of the natural law from the Stoics to the modern church fathers, and to the uses Karl Marx made of Hegel's dialectic and the economic doctrines of the Utilitarians. Similarly, the ways of history can trace the development of legal doctrines. They can show the development of the international law of war as it responds to the development and perfection of modern weaponry and new means of destruction.

As political science has moved into a closer alliance with the social and behavioral sciences, however, historical studies have found less favor than they did earlier. Part of the reason has been an informal declaration of independence from the discipline of history; fewer and fewer political scientists (and, indeed, fewer historians) care to think of political science as contemporary history. The reason runs deeper though. The historical mode typically yields only an evolutionary or developmental analysis; that is to say, it can produce explanations and analyses only in terms of time sequences. Sometimes that analysis is necessary and appropriate, but often it is not; and where it has been used for a sort of projective analysis—academic "prediction"—political scientists are increasingly suspicious and wary. Political scientists no longer are eager to make voting projections on the basis of historical data; they would far rather work with sample survey data on individual voting preferences.[7]

The Case Study

The term *case study* refers to the examination of some political unit. That unit may be a single event in all of its ramifications (e.g., the election of 1964 in Britain), a single political organization (the American Medical Association or a local political party), a single governmental institution (a committee, or agency of the United Nations or of a local suburb), or a single decision (the passage of a bill in Congress or the decision of a case in the Supreme Court). Furthermore, the treatment of the unit is of necessity comprehensive rather than selective; it deals with the unit as a whole rather than selected parts of a number of similar cases. It centers on the study of the specific Congressional committee, for example, studying all of its activities and relationships, rather than on some selected aspect (say, the operation of the seniority system) of committees in general.

The attractions of the case study are numerous. Because it covers the entire unit, it has the color and intrinsic interest of fine political journalism. For this reason and for its ability to recreate the realities of the political process the case study flourishes as a teaching device. Through its reporting the student sits close to the congressman, the judge, the President, or the ambassador as, in the pages of the case study, he makes the decision again. Case studies also provide descriptive materials which suggest relationships for more precise analysis. They lead to studies more precise in their theoretical propositions and the testing of them. So, one finds a number of fields in political science passing through a "case-study phase" which is usually followed by more theoretical comparative and co-variate studies.

The advantages of the case study are also its disadvantages, however. Since it is concerned with a single unit, one cannot gen-

---

[7] Historical studies in American political science are typified by Carl B. Swisher's *American Constitutional Development* (Boston: Houghton Mifflin Company, 1954) and Charles H. McIlwain, *The Growth of Political Thought in the West* (New York: The Macmillan Company, 1932).

eralize from it. Generalization is possible only if there is a number of similar case studies, and scholars unhappily have a frustrating individualism that works against their following the mold of an earlier case study. Furthermore, although the descriptive details may be endlessly fascinating, the case study has real analytical limits precisely because of that descriptiveness. A study of the litigating of a single case before the courts—with details about the parties, the events which led to the litigation, the attorneys, the evidence of the trial, the argument before appellate courts, and the consequences of the decision—may show a great deal about how the judicial process operates in one instance. One cannot, however, infer from it generalizations about the judicial process in large numbers of cases; even less can one infer *why* courts act and decide as they do.[8]

Comparative Studies

At one time in the development of American political science, comparative studies were little more than descriptions of foreign governments. They were "comparative" only in the sense of an implicit comparison with the American political system. But this is no longer so. Contemporary political scientists compare institutions, such as parties or legislatures; processes, such as those of socialization or conflict-resolution; and even whole political systems. Comparative studies differ, too, in their range. Some extend the comparison across national boundaries, or even across cultural boundaries; some, such as a recent four-state study of the legislative process in the United States, cross neither.

In many ways the flocking to comparative studies indicates our inability to control political variables. Having at hand a stable political system with a high standard of living, the political scientist cannot create one with impoverished millions. He can only seek some other political system with a similar stability and a different standard of living. In his comparisons, therefore, he seeks similarity in those variables he wants to hold constant and difference in those in which he seeks variation. The greater the similarity between the political systems or parts of systems he is comparing, the greater the number of variables he can hold constant—but the narrower the range of the generalizations he can make. As he decreases the similarity—as

---

8 Two well-known and excellent case studies are Stephen K. Bailey, *Congress Makes a Law* (New York: Columbia University Press, 1950) and Bernard C. Cohen, *The Political Process and Foreign Policy: The Making of the Japanese Peace Settlement* (Princeton, N.J.: Princeton University Press, 1957).

he takes, for instance, the Western and non-Western systems—he opens up the possibility of a greater range of difference and a greater range of possible explanations; but he also runs the risk that variables not identified by his study are in fact main contributors to similarities and differences which he finds.

Whatever the scope of their work, the comparers are in many ways the new "general theorists" of political science. They have freed American political science from its parochial attention to the governments and politics of only the Western world. They seek generalizations about all political systems, regardless of national and cultural boundaries. They search for general patterns of politics which transcend time and place; they seek elements common to all political systems and those which vary with culture and experience. The scholars who limit themselves to one or a few Western governments deal with political systems built on cultures and societies which are relatively similar; but those who expand it to non-Western systems can more easily get to certain fundamental social factors underlying the political system and its variations—to the kinship system, the family, the basic social structure, and the nature of the economy. The inclusion of primitive and developing political systems in comparative analysis is to political science what a new, more powerful telescope is to astronomy—it expands the range and scope of the inquiry.[9]

Co-variate Analysis

Although this term is less widely used in political science than the others, political scientists do often think of a kind of research strategy which focuses on the relationship between or among a small number of variables within a single political system. Their literature abounds with studies which show the relationship between the forms of local governments and the characteristics of the cities in which they are found, between personality characteristics and the political attitudes of American adults, between socio-economic tensions and the incidence of aggressive national acts.

---

[9] John Wahlke, Heinz Eulau, William Buchanan, and LeRoy Ferguson in *The Legislative System* (New York: John Wiley & Sons, Inc., 1962) have compared the legislative process and legislative roles in four American states; Gabriel Almond and Sidney Verba's *The Civic Culture* (Princeton, N.J.: Princeton University Press, 1963) crosses both national and cultural boundaries to study the political cultures of Mexico, Italy, Germany, Great Britain, and the United States. As a final illustration one can list Oliver P. Williams and Charles R. Adrian, *Four Cities: A Study in Comparative Policy Making* (Philadelphia: University of Pennsylvania Press, 1963).

In studies such as these the work of the political scientist is characterized by theoretical confidence. He states a hypothesis that a probable relationship exists, and he collects his data in terms of it. Here the perimeters of the study are defined not by time, events, or institutions, but by dependent and independent variables—by, in other words, what the scholar expects to find. He has a fairly firm hunch about what he will find; and his research strategy is, therefore, pointed and directed to it. It is the closest of these modes of research to the traditional outlines of the scientific method. Since it is possible only in a discipline fairly confident of its hypotheses, it is fairly new to a political science which is just beginning to harvest its first theoretical propositions.

Unless one combines such a strategy with the comparative approach, it is limited to one political system, and its findings can be validated only by other studies in other political systems. That is its greatest problem. A problem, too, is the commitment one makes in the basic design: the advance gamble one makes on a limited range of inquiry. If the relationship or cause is not, contrary to expectations, among the ones projected, then we can say no more than that A, B, C, and D do not explain or relate to F or G. When one shoots at precise theoretical targets, he cannot use a blunderbuss. He must, therefore, be pretty sure of his aim.[10]

These, then, are the skills, the approaches, and the scholarly commitments of American political science. The following two chapters describe briefly what they have yielded.

---

[10] These works in all their variation may be suggested by Karl Deutsch, *Nationalism and Social Communication* (Cambridge, Mass.: The M.I.T. Press, 1953) and by Julius Turner's *Party and Constituency* (Baltimore: Johns Hopkins University Press, 1952).

The Individual
and the
Political System

chapter four

A large and complex political system, like a piece of great sculpture, cannot be fully viewed and comprehended from any single perspective. A political scientist may study the political behavior of individuals; but if he so restricts himself, he runs the risk of missing the entirety of the political system as it brings together and arbitrates the political demands of millions of individuals. On the other hand, to look only at the totality of politics takes one's eye away from the individual whose wishes, interests, and demands are the raw materials of politics which the system ultimately "processes."

Perhaps we can borrow the terms of economics—which faces the same problem of describing the whole and the parts—and refer to "micropolitics" and "macropolitics." The micropolitical view is the look at the individual and his attempts to influence the operation of the system. From that perspective we see the trees rather than the forest, but it is a necessary perspective if we are to learn anything of the nature and composition of the forest. The macropolitical view is that of the entire system, an "aerial view," so to speak, of the operation of the entire political system as it copes with the political behavior of individuals and aggregates of individuals within it.

THE WORLD OF MICROPOLITICS

Basic to the operation of the political system are the demands, the aspirations, the attitudes of the individual members of the society. These political "raw materials" may be the goals and demands of the citizen; they may be the concepts he holds of his responsibility to and place in the political system; or they may be the norms by which he judges the operation of the system. Whatever they are, they become

39

important when the individual takes political action on their behalf—that is, when he makes them an overt goal for public policy and seeks to turn policy in their direction. The citizen may strongly disapprove of alcoholic beverages; to achieve the goal of their rejection, he may work through religious organizations or temperance societies; but he may also join a prohibitionist political party or seek legal prohibition of the sale or consumption of alcoholic drinks. With that decision to seek political means for his goals he enters the stream of political activity.

Each political individual comes into the political arena with a full set of these goals—they range from proposals for prayer in the public schools to legislation preventing discrimination in employment. He possesses political attitudes beyond these policy goals, however. He has some sort of understanding about the political system, some knowledge of it and of how the individual acts and operates within it. Obviously the individual's political effectiveness will not be great if his knowledge level is not sufficient to tell him that his property taxes are set locally rather than by the state government. He also has a view of himself in the political system. He has attitudes which define his own political role and which appraise the usefulness and efficacy of his political action. Nothing quite dampens political participation as fast as beliefs that "one vote doesn't make any difference," or "my feelings don't count, anyway."

All his attitudes and orientations to politics result from the individual's social experience. They are learned in the same way he learns about other social relationships and institutions. Some of them may be taught formally in civics courses, but most of them result from his everyday group affiliations—group experiences all the way from his family ties to his membership in a professional, business, or labor organization. Members of business and labor groups often have sharply different policy goals—support of and opposition to "right to work" laws, for example; but they just as often have sharply different evaluations of government itself. They may differ over the proper role of government and over the efficacy of "states' rights."

The complex process of the acquisition of these goals and perceptions about the political system is most frequently referred to as "political socialization." It is a process vastly more complex than political scientists would have said a few years ago. In the first place, although one can learn directly about politics, some socialization results from transfer from nonpolitical situations; habits of discussion and participation in schools, homes, and clubs may be transferred to the political system. Then, although the process begins early in life—one recent study indicates that children have well-formed ideas about political authority by the age of ten or twelve—it goes on continuously through life. At crucial times in life, such as when he leaves home to go to college or when he retires at sixty-five, the individual may actually undergo a "resocialization" process. Furthermore, throughout life we constantly acquire new political roles, shifting in and out of party work, becoming more or less regular voters. In fact, political organizations such as parties and interest groups have as one of their prime goals the partial resocialization of their members.[1]

Given this social acquisition of our goals and roles in the political system, it is not surprising that differences in individual political behavior are primarily related to differences in social characteristics. In every political system the better-educated, higher socio-economic status groups are more active in political organizations, more apt to vote, more apt to participate in any way in the political system. Even the goals of activity relate to social characteristics. As Seymour Lipset has pointed out, party preferences of adults in industrial societies fall predominantly along social and economic class lines. Political activity and participation is greater among men than among women, too, largely because of lingering tendencies to identify the home as woman's proper place. Political inactivity and withdrawal is associated with low social and economic status and with a consequent sense of alienation from the community and a feeling of powerlessness in it. The residents of shantytown or a racial ghetto may well feel that their political activity would have no effect and that they have no important stake in the community.[2]

The participating, politically active man and woman also are characterized by harmony and homogeneity in their political attitudes and values. One's political decision is easiest when all of his signs and cues point in the same direction—when, for example, his family's party preference agrees with that of his occupational group and his fellow workers. By our selection of social experiences we tend to buttress such a political homogeneity. We select friends and reading material with political points of view similar to ours. But crosscutting of political allegiances and roles may nonetheless occur. Consider the case of the young woman raised in a Republican family who marries

---

[1] See, for example, Herbert Hyman, *Political Socialization* (New York: Free Press of Glencoe, Inc., 1958) and Robert Lane, *Political Life* (New York: Free Press of Glencoe, Inc., 1959).

[2] Lipset's *Political Man* (New York: Doubleday & Company, Inc., 1959) exemplifies the sociological study of politics.

a life-long Democrat—or the case of the Catholic schoolteacher whose religious ties dispose her to favor some federal aid to parochial schools but whose professional association, the National Education Association, opposes it. In such cases of crosscutting cues or pressures within the individual, we know that a lessening of political activity or participation often results. An escape from politics may seem the only solution to such internal political conflict.[3]

Recent studies, however, indicate that the individual's political behavior may be related to psychological and personality variables as well as to social characteristics. Although the theories of Sigmund Freud have won surprisingly little favor with political scientists, many scholars have accepted the concept of the "authoritarian personality," despite its Freudian derivation. That is to say, they recognize a personality syndrome which exhibits paranoid suspicions, a fear and rejection of "outsiders," and an inability to tolerate uncertainty and complexity. These people quite naturally seek structure, authority, and leadership in their social relationships. Other more recent studies have related personality characteristics such as anomie, pessimism, and alienation to a conservative political ideology. (It is interesting to note, parenthetically, that scholars in their concern for the political consequences of "deviant" personality characteristics have largely ignored the politics of more typical personalities.) Just on the common-sense level, it stands to reason that the political behavior of a neurotic person with persecution feelings or deep resentments will be affected by them, just as his nonpolitical behavior will.[4]

In the first chapter (Figure 1) we visualized the entire political process as beginning with the individual and his political awareness and ending with the making of public policy. In between these two end points there occurs a multifaceted process of organizing individuals into ever greater political aggregates. The individual possesses only miniscule political influence, but in majorities he can move the machinery of government. Yet the organization even of democratic majorities is not a single process triggered by periodic elections; it is instead a series of organizing and cumulating processes going on simultaneously.

The mobilization of interests may in the local community fall to informal social and economic elites. Especially at the local com-

---

[3] For an excellent analysis of conflicting social pressures in and on the individual, see David B. Truman, *The Governmental Process* (New York: Alfred A. Knopf, Inc., 1951).

[4] T. W. Adorno *et al.*, *The Authoritarian Personality* (New York: Harper & Row, 1950). See also Eric Hoffer, *The True Believer* (New York: Harper & Row, 1951).

munity level the socio-economic power of the community's elite can be more easily converted into political power. These local elites—the comparative few who control wealth and status—enjoy the social acceptance ánd community leadership which people will follow. They often control local employment and investment, the local newspaper and other channels of political information; and through trusted lieutenants they often control the local party organizations. They frequently are pillars of local country-club society and old stalwarts of the Rotary Club and chamber of commerce. Their ability to influence others in the local community is not, therefore, difficult to understand. The more simple and homogeneous a local society, the easier it is to convert social and economic influence to political influence, for in such communities there are rarely competing elites or alternative nuclei around which to build political aggregates. Some writers have argued that single national elites control even the political systems of great nations. The Marxists so argue about the economic elite, and C. Wright Mills described a single "power elite" dominating the American system. Few political scientists would agree. They see instead in any large country or even in any large city a number of political elites which have selective and limited political goals and which negotiate and conflict with each other. Different elites may control decisions on public education and the planning of new expressways; and, what is more, they may come from different social and economic groups in the community.[5]

The greatest bulk of the mobilizing of political individuals, however, is carried on by political parties and interest groups. Most interest groups only occasionally venture into politics; they may, like the American Bar Association or the American Medical Association, seek most of their goals through nonpolitical avenues. Only occasionally, in the case of proposals for government health insurance or for altering a state's criminal code, do they enter politics. The political party, on the other hand, functions only as an organizer of political influence. That is to say, it seeks only political means for its goals, most particularly the means of contesting elections. Yet both are large, loose organizations with similar problems and limitations as mobilizers of political individuals. Both have difficulties in maintaining internal democracy, for the capture and use of the party or interest group by a skilled and interested minority is no rarer than it is in a PTA or fraternal organization.

---

[5] See C. Wright Mills, *The Power Elite* (New York: Oxford University Press, 1956). Among the studies of local political power perhaps the finest is Robert Dahl, *Who Governs?* (New Haven: Yale University Press, 1961).

Both, too, face serious problems of internal cohesion and solidarity, for none of them command the complete and undivided loyalties of their members. The individual who joins the party or interest group has other group memberships, other loyalties, which may conflict. He may be brought together in a political party with men of vastly different outlooks on many issues; the party may indeed have attracted men for reasons (such as the personal appeal of a magnetic leader or the political affiliation of one's father) having nothing at all to do with issues. If, for example, the individual is an American Legionnaire he may find that his fellow Legionnaires differ on federal aid to education and American policy toward Cuba and Latin America. So the building of these aggregates of influence is not easy. Incipient differences within any party or interest group limit the range of its political activity and the forthrightness of its stands. So great is the variety of goals and interests of a populace as heterogeneous as the American that as an organization builds larger and larger aggregates—aiming ultimately for a majority—it of necessity recruits into itself a greater range of limiting and debilitating differences. The result one political scientist has called a "law of imperfect political mobilization." [6]

Scholarly explorations into individual political behavior have not been common. An exception would be a challenging recent work by Gabriel Almond and Sidney Verba, entitled appropriately *The Civic Culture*.[7] It is a study of political attitudes in five countries: Italy, Germany, Great Britain, Mexico, and the United States. Using national cross samples which totalled about 5,000 individuals, the authors got their data through structured interviews of about an hour carried out by respected polling organizations in those countries. Then they conducted second, follow-up interviews with individuals who on the basis of their first interviews seemed to exemplify certain "types" of citizens. The citizens of the samples were asked about their perception of the political system and their part in it—what impact, for instance, did they think that government had on their everyday lives; what obligation did they feel to participate in politics; and what kind of treatment would they expect to get from a government bureaucrat?

---

[6] See E. E. Schattschneider, *Party Government* (New York: Holt, Rinehart & Winston, Inc., 1942) for a discussion of the internal problems of the American parties. See also Angus Campbell *et al.*, *The American Voter* (New York: John Wiley & Sons, Inc., 1960); Harmon Zeigler, *Interest Groups in American Society* (Englewood Cliffs, N.J.: Prentice-Hall, Inc., 1964); and Frank J. Sorauf, *Political Parties in the American System* (Boston: Little, Brown and Company, 1964).

[7] Princeton: Princeton University Press, 1963.

The conclusions and findings of the book are too subtle and too varied even to begin to summarize. Many relationships emerge from the combination of attitudes and political histories—for example, the better educated the individual, the greater impact he sees his government having on him. From the welter of findings emerge, however, five portraits of five quite different political cultures.

The Italian culture is one of political alienation, low feelings of national pride, distrust of government, and little sense of obligation to it. In Mexico the authors find a combination of alienation and aspiration. Mixed with national pride and acceptance of the political system are cynical views about government's unfairness and ineffectiveness. Mexicans have a high self-appraisal of their political competence, and yet they are relatively inactive in political deed. The German civic culture, on the other hand, is marked by knowledge of the political system and activity in it and by confidence in its fairness. Yet, Germans are rarely active in political groups and other informal kinds of political activity. As the authors point out, the orientation of Germans to their political system is one "of the subject rather than the participant." The American political culture is labelled a "participant civic culture." Its citizens are politically active and frequently exposed to politics, and they are involved personally and emotionally in the events of politics. Finally, a "deferential civic culture" marks Britain. As in the United States participation, exposure to politics, involvement, and a sense of competence is high. Yet, the British have maintained a deference to the authority of government not found in the United States.

A preoccupation with political individuals and their "civic culture," however, fails to account for the ultimate resolution of their political contestings. It gives one no picture of the operation of those special institutions of government through which most larger political systems operate. To that total picture of the political system as a great political arbiter we now turn.

THE MAKING OF PUBLIC POLICY

At the very heart of the political system is the making of public policy—those authoritative decisions which carry out and enforce the wishes of the influential in the political system. Expressions of public policy include laws, judicial decisions, treaties, executive rules and orders, local ordinances, administrative decisions—or any rule of conduct behind which stands the enforcing power of the political system. Consequently, a very wide range of public officials makes public policy. Legislatures do so most obviously; but so does an administrative official when he decides that in filing income-tax returns, memberships in country clubs may not be deducted as legitimate costs of doing business. So also does the judge who gives specific meaning to the vague constitutional words "due process of law." In fact, it is one of the inescapable facts of twentieth-century government that a decreasing percentage of public policy is made today by legislatures.

Not only is the making of public policy the very center of political operations; it is also the most manageable and useful point at which to examine the total political system. In the making of public policy one sees the channeling of all the influences in the political system. All the strivings of individuals and groups are ultimately directed at influencing the making of public policy. Influence, indeed, may be defined as the ability to select decision-makers or to shape the ways in which they act. The mobilization of voters by the political parties, the lobbying and proselytizing of interest groups, the activities of individuals and powerful elites—all of these converge on the decision-makers as they hammer out public policies. Or, to look at it another way, the political system as a totality, acting through these decision-makers, must choose among competing demands and interests brought to bear within it. Different parties, interest groups, and individuals want the political machinery to enforce *their* norms, enact *their* public-welfare programs, or prefer *their* interests over others. The choice among these competing and conflicting interests is made in the very process of enacting public policy.

The kinds of influences impinging on the work of decision-makers do not differ materially whether the decision-makers are legislators, executives, judges, or administrators. Basically they can be put into three main categories: those within the individual decision-maker, those within the decision-making group, and those from outside the group.

Influences Within the Individual

These are the pressures within rather than on the individual decision-makers. For illustrative purposes, let us take the United States Supreme Court. Frequently in interpreting the vague phrases of the constitution or of some statute a justice may have to make choices among reasonable alternatives, just as a congressman or President must do. Even the sincerest devotion to detached justice and the supremacy of law will not free him from the burdens of choice; and in making those policy decisions he is subjected to the same kinds of influences as are other political decision-makers.

To the business of judging, the member of the Court will bring his own social and political values, first of all. In 1964 the Supreme Court had to decide a series of cases on the constitutionality of legislative apportionment within the states. For such a question there is no precedent and little guide in the intention of the framers of the constitution. Parties in the case argue different theories of representation—one man, one vote, or the wisdom of representing units of government and area as well as sheer population—but the judge may ultimately have to dip into some personal intellectual reservoir for a decision. Or, to take another example, a large number of the justices of the Supreme Court in the last generation have had experience as high-level administrators in government; they have been governors, Cabinet members, members of regulatory commissions. With their greater knowledge of the administrative processes and its problems they may very well be more sympathetic to the exercise of administrative discretion than some justice who has had no administrative experience. All of this is not to say that a judge's personal values and experience are relevant to every case he decides, nor is it even to say that those values prevail even where they are relevant; but they may. History and scholarship have shown cases in which they have. The great division in the Supreme Court in the 1930's pitted justices who had grown up in urban, industrial states (New York, Pennsylvania, and Massachusetts) against those from the western frontier (Utah, Wyoming, Tennessee, and Minnesota). The former group was far more willing to concede the constitutionality of social welfare legislation and regulations of the economy; the latter held tightly to values of individual initiative and laissez-faire capitalism.

No single element of the decision-maker's own perceptual apparatus is more important than his own definition of his role as a decision-maker. The role that the justice of the Supreme Court envisions for himself depends in part on his philosophy of the law and of the judge's part in its creation and evolution, in part on his perception of the relationship of the Court to the rest of government, and in part on his view of the place of the appointive judiciary in a democracy. In fact, there rages on the Supreme Court today a battle between two role positions. The "activists," typified by Chief Justice Warren and Justices Black and Douglas, see the Court as an instrument of social change and innovation; they favor the Court's using all of its impressive powers to give contemporary meaning to the constitution. The school of "self-restraint," typified recently by Justices Frankfurter and Harlan, would be less active lest they create enemies for the Court or undermine the popularly chosen branches of government; they favor a more restricted role for the Court in constitutional and statutory interpretation.[8]

Influences Within the Decision-Making Group

To continue our illustration, the justices of the Supreme Court function not as isolated individual decision-makers but as members of a group in which the individuals interact with each other in the decision-making process and in which the well-being of the group must also be considered. Indeed, no single factor explains as much of the history of the Supreme Court as its concern for its own safety and well-being, its independence and influence, in the American political system.

These intragroup influences begin with the influence of individuals on other individual decision-makers—of justice on justice and Chief Justice on justices. One justice may be more experienced on certain questions; for example, Justice Douglas, having been an early chairman of the Securities and Exchange Commission, possesses an expertise on financial matters that must surely command the attention of his fellow justices. We know, too, from the correspondence of Justice Holmes that he respected and heeded the economic expertise of his younger colleague, Louis Brandeis. The work of a justice may also be influenced by staff aids, their clerks, who assist and work on the peripheries of the group. These young men, who come to the Court just after completing brilliant careers in law school, may bring new ideas to the Court from the law schools' scholars. They may, too, help the justices review petitions of litigants who would like the Court to take their cases. Even though the decisions are ultimately the justices', the clerks may introduce ideas and information that might never have been introduced in their absence.

Above all, however, the group, the organization itself, exerts an incalculable force on policy-making. The individual justice must observe the norms and traditions of the Supreme Court. He must give great weight to precedent; he must observe the unwritten policies of the Court (e.g., the tradition that the Court will if at all possible decide a case on nonconstitutional rather than constitutional grounds);

---

[8] Attitude studies of American decision-makers include Duncan MacRae, *Dimensions of Congressional Voting* (Berkeley: University of California Press, 1958) and Glendon Schubert, *Quantitative Analysis of Judicial Behavior* (New York: Free Press of Glencoe, Inc., 1959). Charles Clapp's *The Congressman—His Work as He Sees It* (Washington: The Brookings Institution, 1963) is also very relevant.

and he must work within the expectation of judicial dignity and detachment. He must, as one judge put it, accept the "cult of the robe"; but more than that, he must guard the power, the prestige, and the well-being of the Court itself. He must worry about incursions on its domain by a Congress which has the power to alter its jurisdiction, to fix the number of members on the Court, and to grant its administrative budget. The justices can hardly forget that the post-Civil War Congress literally carved the cases challenging Reconstruction from the Court's jurisdiction or that Congress came close in the late 1930's to "packing" the Court. Furthermore, the Supreme Court must collectively be concerned over its ability to win either acceptance for its decisions or Presidential commitment to enforce them. The Court has no real enforcement power, and it cannot afford the indignity of being defied or ignored.[9]

Influences Outside the Group

These are the influences we most commonly think of, the "pressures" from nonparticipants in the decision-making process. Congress has its "lobbyists," and so in a limited way does the Supreme Court. Powerful interest groups manage much of the litigation that raises great constitutional issues before the Court. The National Association for the Advancement of Colored People brought the cases in which the Supreme Court ended legal segregation in public education in 1954, and three large national groups (the American Civil Liberties Union, the American Jewish Congress, and Protestants and Other Americans United) have organized and financed many of the recent cases on the issue of the separation of church and state. In other words, the influence of these groups is conveyed to the Court, not by buttonholing the justices in the lobbies of the Supreme Court building, but by framing issues and legal questions, by the presentation of legal alternatives and argument to the Court.

Although the Court does not feel the influence of political parties and home-town districts, as members of Congress do, the justices must attend to other external influences. Leaders of the bar and legal scholarship cannot go unnoted; they lead and control a professional opinion which is responsible for the judgment accorded the Court by its legal peers. Justices, just like stonemasons, like to be respected and admired by their fellow craftsmen. They also feel the influence of the

---

[9] The general literature on organizational theory and the internal behavior of large organizations has increasingly influenced the study of decision-making groups in political science. Typical of these works is Amitai Etzioni's *A Comparative Analysis of Complex Organizations* (New York: Free Press of Glencoe, Inc., 1961).

mass media, powerful elites, and individuals who paint the image of the Court and very much determine its popular acceptance. Finally, the Court, as is any decision-making body, is the subject of constant influences from other governmental bodies. A President, such as Franklin Roosevelt, may take his case against the Court to radio, television, or the press conference. He may, as Roosevelt did, castigate it (". . . a horse and buggy Court"). Recently, too, the Court has felt the sting of criticism from the Conference of State Chief Justices for what they thought was an abandonment of the principles of judicial self-restraint.

Illustration of these categories of influence could be drawn easily from legislature and executives, too. In fact, a goodly share of the scholarly literature of decision-making deals with legislatures. Stephen K. Bailey's *Congress Makes a Law*,[10] for example, follows a single bill, the Full Employment Act of 1946, through the legislative labyrinths, showing not only the actions of Congress but the many influences on its decision-making—those operating "in" as well as "on" the congressmen. The picture Bailey paints is of a series of crucial decisions on the bill rather than any one decisive action. Other scholars, such as Donald Matthews in *U. S. Senators and Their World*,[11] have focused on the decision-making apparatus itself. Based on personal observation and interviews with senators, their staffs, journalists, and lobbyists, the Matthews book describes the men and behavior of the Senate from 1947–1957. Matthews deals with, among other topics, the social characteristics of the Senators (one-half are lawyers, for instance), their political careers and experience (again, a majority have been in government and politics for most of their adult lives), the folkways of the Senate (the demands for an almost Victorian deference and courtesy), the activities of lobbyists (the likelihood of their being influenced by Senators, as well as vice versa), and senatorial decision-making (the Senators who don't "go along" with the majority and who vote with small and hopeless minorities also fail to conform to Senate folkways and fail in general effectiveness as Senators). Matthews conveys a general impression of a decision-making institution which is not only responsive to outside influences and political realities but which at the same time works hard to maintain its own organizational health and internal harmony.

More recently four American political scientists have carried the study of the legislative process to the state level. They interviewed

---

10 New York: Columbia University Press, 1950.
11 Chapel Hill: University of North Carolina Press, 1960.

legislators in four American states (Ohio, California, Tennessee, and New Jersey) to analyze the roles these legislators saw themselves playing in the legislative process of their state. The four-state comparison also enabled the authors to control for a number of political differences (such as the degree of two-party competitiveness) among the four states. Their findings suggested that legislative roles vary with, among other factors, the party and factional composition of the state, the legislator's perception of his own effectiveness, the stage of his political career, and the general political culture and expectations of the legislative chamber. The authors also found that legislators actually possess patterns of roles rather than a single, all-pervasive legislative role. For example, the rural legislator may assume one role in his dealings with people from his home county and quite another in the tightly knit group life of his fellow legislators.[12]

It would be both convenient and comforting if one could relate this macropolitical decision-making process easily to the political individual and to what we have called micropolitics. Such is not the case, however; for the process of mobilizing and conveying political consensus from the individual in Ashtabula to the United States Congress is vastly more complex than most Americans realize. Indeed, we tend to perceive and distort it through some essentially apolitical or antipolitical attitudes. We search for the man above politics, the "Washington myth"; and we fervently hope that decisions will be made in a political vacuum, away from the press and strain of powerful political influences. It appears that we would often prefer to think of the Congress as a group of uncommitted men examining each public issue afresh and arriving at policy decisions with the earnestness of a college debating society. We like also to think of the individual's relationship to government as a simple and direct one, free from the corrupting intermediary services of "amoral" politicians and "pressure groups." The reality of the workings of a political system, for better or for worse, scarcely fits such hopes and stereotypes.

In the first place, all individuals in the political system, whether they be the occasional voter or the senatorial leader, come to it with a heavy commitment to certain values and ways of doing things. Even the thoughtful man does not approach a political decision as a *tabula rasa*, or as a completely open-minded individual prepared to assess the equities all over again. The individual American voter, for example, has a heavy and unchanging commitment to one party; and that standing commitment will decide the Presidential vote of 80 or

---

[12] John Wahlke, Heinz Eulau, William Buchanan, and LeRoy Ferguson, *The Legislative System* (New York: John Wiley & Sons, Inc., 1962).

90 per cent of the voters, quite regardless of who the candidates are or what the burning issues are. Congressmen, too, may be so committed to a point of view that the cagey interest group knows that its chances of changing commitments are not great; hence, these groups spend most of their time activating and reinforcing commitment rather than trying to alter it. Perhaps this degree of commitment is necessary; few of us have the time or the energy to decide every issue without falling back on old cues. Perhaps, too, these long-run commitments lend a necessary stability to the political system; they will, for example, see a political party over bad days and prevent it from being wiped out. They do, however, limit and restrict what powerful aggregates of influence can accomplish at any one time.

These aggregates coming up through the system to try to shape the making of public policy encounter another limitation. Not all of them have equal entree to decision-makers. The fact that lawyers dominate the legislatures of the United States means, among other things, that they will give greater attention and respect to lawyers, their interests, and their legal arguments. In this case the pattern of influence within the group determines who from the outside will have greater access. Sometimes it is an institutional fact that governs access. The existence of unlimited debate in the Senate, with the consequent threat of a filibuster, has reduced the effective access of the Negro in the Congress. Groups such as those representing the Negro and American labor feel that their Congressional access is poor and seek, therefore, to influence other decision-makers to which they enjoy better access. Hence, the Negro interest groups have gone to the courts, and labor has increasingly begun to operate through the parties and in elections.

Furthermore, despite fairly widespread adult suffrage and extensive political freedom, not all people and not all groups enjoy equal political influence. The process of influencing policy begins with all the individual contestants on the same starting line, but from there on the race is to the swift. The ability to develop influence in the political system depends first of all on economic and social resources. "Politics ain't beanbag," said the estimable Mr. Dooley; and it costs dearly to play it, especially in a day of campaigning and influence through the mass media. So, too, social status marks a political cause with respectability and prestige, and a candidate with "acceptance" and reliability. Just the sheer numbers of individuals gathered into the aggregate will alter its influence, if only because numbers can in most cases (one exception being the American Negro) be converted into votes in open elections. Political skills and knowledge also help a group maximize its political effectiveness. For this reason many interest groups are eager to hire former congressmen (often at salaries greater than they earned as congressmen) to serve as their representatives before the Congress. The former congressmen bring to them both access and skills. Finally, one might mention the intensity of the group's commitment to its interest. How much of their "political currency" are the members willing to spend on the cause? How much time, money, attention will they give? How strong an organization will they build and maintain? Will they submerge other issues that could divide them? Consumer groups in the United States exemplify low-intensity interest and, therefore, relatively limited influence. The consumer—which is to say, each of us—places his interest as a consumer fairly well down on his list of personal causes, and by the time he has acted on higher-priority commitments he can bring little time or dedication or resources to fighting for consumer causes.

Above all, as one views this political system as a whole he must realize that it moves slowly, that there is a stabilizing, conservatizing aspect to political institutions. Policy-making institutions tend, for one thing, to place a high value on their own stability and their own status quo. The administrative agency must always be concerned about protecting its relationships with Congress and the private groups with which it deals if it is to protect its mission. Furthermore, the presence of great opposing aggregates of influence in the system—business and labor, for example—may produce only deadlock and inaction; and as political institutions grow, the decision-making process becomes more and more dispersed. In Congress it is dispersed into a welter of committees and subcommittees. And where power is dispersed the status quo is promoted. If the consent of five power centers is necessary for policy action, one must secure all five to initiate change, but one can block change by securing the consent of one.[13]

Thus in a large and involuted political system such as the American, we have ultimately government by a series of constantly shifting aggregates, each with different goals and with their eyes set on different policy-making centers. On any one issue—as a raise in the tariff on imported Swiss watches—we may have policy decided by the interested and involved minority. It is, to ring a change on Calhoun, government by "concurring minorities." Only rather rarely does the great majority of individuals, and the organizations that represent them, become involved and try to exert influence on a policy-

---

[13] See David Truman's *Governmental Process* for an overview of the American political system. For a contrast, see David Apter, *The Gold Coast in Transition* (Princeton: Princeton University Press, 1955).

making question. Where one finds this kind of majority involvement he often finds the flow of influence reversed. Influence ceases to flow uphill from the "grass roots" individual to the decision-making centers and moves back downhill. Presidents and powerful congressional leaders increasingly bear the burden of organizing great majorities for the decisions they would make. That fact largely explains the challenge and the power of the American Presidency and of political leadership in general.

One last word may be necessary about the decision-making focus. I have for illustrative purposes referred exclusively to the American political system. All of the concepts and relationships discussed above presume the free, open, competitive politics of a democracy. Obviously the analytical model would have to be altered somewhat for a totalitarian political system—but not as much as one ₁ ₁ight think at first blush. In political systems such as that of the Soviet Union, internal pressures operate within the persons of the ruling ₋ligarchy, and the oligarchs interact with each other. Even external pressures—a deeply felt desire for more and better consumer goods, for example—may be transmitted indirectly to the major decision-making bodies. So will the views and wishes of powerful party and military elites. Even totalitarian political systems must depend on popular acceptance and consensus, for no political system can keep a bayonet at every throat.

THE INTERNATIONAL POLITICAL SYSTEM

The international political system is dominated by nation states, all of them jealous of their autonomy (their "sovereignty") and all of them with their own national goals and interests. There is no conflict-settling apparatus with a preponderance of force. In other words, there is no true political system of the sort one finds within the individual nations. Without the arbitrating institutions to resolve conflicting demands, the nations of the international system are thrown into a free-bargaining interplay of influence and national power in which decisions are made according to the coercive capacities of individual nations and alliances. It is "power politics" in its purest form, because success for a nation's goals depends on its ability to enforce them itself.

Because of its special characteristics, the international political system cannot be analyzed in the same terms as a closed political system within a single society. The nature of decision-making is different. Since there are no arbitrating political institutions, there are really no decision-makers. Bargaining and negotiation replace the formalities of policy-making. Furthermore, nations in the international system are not strictly comparable to persons in a political system. They develop goals and decide to take political action in quite different ways.

Given the "untamed," self-enforcing nature of this international political system, the crucial factor continues to be the coercive capacity, the "national power," of the separate nations. That power may take a number of forms, chiefly military power and economic power (e.g., control of the markets for another nation's products). There may also be a far less tangible power of opinion and status—the acceptance and approval of other nations, their populations, and whatever international community of thought may be developing. The important question for international politics remains the explanation of differences in national power. To do so one must examine the bases on which a nation develops its international leverage.

Lists of the determinants of national power differ from scholar to scholar, but there is considerable consensus on many of them. Geographical position can be important, especially if the nation is placed at the entrance to an important waterway, for example. Natural resources, especially reserves of crucial minerals, contribute to national power. So does the sheer number of healthy, productive individuals who live in the nation. Perhaps today the key component is national skills—the technological skills, education, and literacy of the population. Less easy to measure and appraise, but equally important, is the factor of morale. Under its semantic umbrella we may include the cohesiveness and loyalty of the population, its psychological stability, and its sense of purpose and dedication to the nation's international goals. Finally, the stability of a nation's social institutions, its economy, and its political system are crucial. War-making capacity, for example, demands a flexible, adaptive economy and an enormous governmental and private administrative capacity.[14]

National power, however, shifts with an often cruel suddenness. Spain, the scourge of the sixteenth century, fell quickly and dramatically from international dominance. More significantly than any other cause, advances in technology and industrialism alter the nature of national power. Consequently, the millions of young males for army battalions no longer constitute the source of power they once did, nor does Britain's isolation by the English Channel guarantee

---

[14] Klaus Knorr, *The War Potential of Nations* (Princeton, N.J.: Princeton University Press, 1956).

its wartime safety any more. While the bases of national power shift, so also does its relative sufficiency. A nation may rest secure one day in its military supremacy and find it disturbed the next by some other nation's ability to put a man into space or to increase sharply its steel-making capacity.

Those same changes in science and technology have also altered the nature of the skills and instruments of international politics. The most conventional among them has been diplomacy. Long the practice of guarded negotiations among professional, experienced diplomats, it has declined as a combination of innovations in transportation and communication and in the growth of mass, popular government has attracted national leaders and the glare of publicity to diplomatic practice. Various economic instruments—cartels, tariffs, and imperialism—have long been used, too, as instruments of national power. More recently one would have to add economic aid and the threat of its refusal or withdrawal. The instrument of violence, too, has undergone recent shifts. Naked military force and the threat of war has to some extent been replaced by techniques of "half war"—guerrilla infiltration and fomented internal strife. It stymies counter-actions and it carries fewer dangers of retaliation to the nation employing it. Finally, one might mention propaganda and psychological warfare. It is most effective when directed at unstable political systems with a lack of consensus and loyalty—nations such as many of those of Southeast Asia.

Into this system of opposing power capacities there do come stabilizers. A small body of international law has brought stability to some kinds of relations among nations. Growing largely from treaties and custom, it exists because of the willingness of nations to be guided by it, to enforce it on themselves. It is in many ways a law of mutual convenience, and cases come to international tribunals only by the consent of all parties. It is effective, one commentator has said, only because the demands it makes on nations are so light. International organization offers a second stabilizing and integrating element in the international system. An organization such as the United Nations is not, however, a "world government." It has no arbitrative system supported by its own coercive power. Rather the United Nations, and to a lesser extent the regional organizations (such as NATO), are collective security organizations which attempt to countermand the use of military power by building a preponderance of power so great as to deter any possible aggressor. Additionally, they have attempted cautiously to advance the integration of nations in the international system—to bring them into closer cooperation and mutual reliance—

by attacking common problems, such as those of poverty, disease, and illiteracy.[15]

Recently, too, Morton Kaplan has suggested that the international system may have some self-regulative properties, that it may develop stable patterns of relationships among the nations of the system. He begins his book *System and Process in International Politics*[16] by identifying some of those patterns. The classic pattern, of course, is the balance of power, in which all nations act as individuals, each maximizing its own national power while opposing the attempts of any other nation or coalition to dominate the system. He also identifies several varieties of bipolar patterns; in those, two great blocs, each cohering around a single, powerful nation, dominate the international system. Important variations, however, depend on whether the two blocs have reached a rigid choosing-up of sides in which all nations are in one bloc or the other, or whether there remain supranational authorities (such as the UN) or neutral nations which can mediate between the two blocs. In a chilling insight into the possibilities of modern warfare, Kaplan suggests also the possibility of what he calls the "unit veto international system," characterized by a grand stand-off in which the chief nations or blocs possess weapons capable of destroying any other that attacks them, even though they cannot prevent their own destruction.

Each of these patterns Kaplan treats as a type of international system; each is an autonomous, stability-seeking set of relationships among nations. He views these systems as almost organic in their ability to adjust to new stresses within the system. Like the self-regulating classical economy of Adam Smith, each of these systems tends constantly to equilibrium and balance and stability, impelled by some "unseen hand." A major task of the Kaplan work is to suggest how these various models of the international system react to their own tensions and to those from the outside, and how they adapt or fail to adapt to them. His is an attempt, in other words, to describe the international system as a whole, a unity, a structure, and a regulatory mechanism to the relations among nations.

Historical evidence is greatest about the balance-of-power system. From that evidence one can suggest some generalizations about the operation of the balance of power. For example, the small number of essential nations in the balance is one of the key factors leading

---

[15] For these topics and the more general subject of international politics the reader is generally urged to consult Hans Morgenthau, *Politics Among Nations* (New York: Alfred A. Knopf, Inc., 1960).

[16] New York: John Wiley & Sons, Inc., 1957.

to its disintegration. Their paucity decreases the possibility for shift and maneuver, and thus for "balancing," within the system. Furthermore, since the balance of power is the product of competitive relations among nations, each one must constantly try to anticipate the behavior of the others. That necessity in turn results in an overalertness to hostile action and in international suspicion and paranoia. In many ways the position of a nation in the balance of power system is that of a poker-player in a game with stakes higher than he can afford to lose. He must be nerveless and wary, and he must play his cards very close to his vest. That tight-lipped secrecy, however, becomes increasingly difficult for democracies which are expected to explain and defend their strategies and tactics before legislatures and voting publics.

These, then, are some of the ways in which individuals, aggregates of individuals, and even nations act politically. No effort has been made here to judge the value or worth or morality of these activities. The question of normative evaluation will be raised in the following chapter.

The Quest
for the
Political Ideal

chapter five

American political science has developed something of a split personality. On the one hand, its new alliance with the empirical social sciences has committed it to a pursuit of empirical, "factual" knowledge and ultimately to explanatory theories of the political system. On the other hand, however, the study of politics has long been concerned with questions of the good life, of political goals and ethics, and of the "best" forms of government. So, contemporary political science continues to be both science and philosophy, balancing two rather different missions and two sharply contrasting methodologies.

That dual mission concerns two great worlds of knowledge: the world of fact (the "is") and that of value (the "ought"). Although they cannot be completely separated, most political scientists agree there are good and ample reasons for trying. Different scholarly methods and procedures prevail in each. The scholar determines facts, and generalizations about facts, by empirical methods of observation. Not so with values. One cannot "prove" that human equality is "good" in the same way that one demonstrates the causes of political inactivity. Indeed, delineating the ways in which one goes about determining whether equality is or is not "good," or whether democracy is superior to totalitarian dictatorships, furnishes the chief task of this chapter. Furthermore, the separation of the "is" and the "ought" can be justified in terms of differences in the goals of analysis. Analysis of the world of the "is," as was suggested in the last chapter, is directed to explanation of causes and functioning; but analysis of the "ought" justifies, clarifies, and defines optimum conditions and desired ends. It is concerned with applying ethical standards to the operation and the policy decisions of the political system. For these reasons, then, it makes a difference whether one raises a question of fact or one of

59

values, and it makes a supreme difference whether one knows which he is raising. If failure marks this basic distinction, the rest is chaos.

Within American political science an old division of labor has helped to maintain the separation between the "is" and the "ought." The study of political values, norms, ethics—whatever one prefers to call them—has traditionally been in the hands of the "political theorists." Their approach has chiefly been the study of the seminal and influential ideas of Western civilization. Increasingly, however, the two scholarly "personalities" within the profession have begun to bring their considerations closer together. Their *rapprochement* has not resulted from any desire to blur the distinctions between the "is" and the "ought." It results rather from a growing feeling that the strict dichotomy between the "is" and the "ought" is an oversimplification of a complicated, intertwined relationship. Perhaps something of that complexity will be more apparent if we examine the matter of justifying democracy over other forms of government.

DEMOCRACY: THE PROBLEM OF ANALYSIS

The story is told that as the American authoress Gertrude Stein lay dying in Paris one of her friends and proteges pressed close to her and with troubled emotion whispered, "Gertrude, what is the answer to life?" The poet is said to have thought for a moment and then replied serenely, "No, no—what are the *questions?*"

The key to scholarly discovery and philosophical analysis is in asking the right questions. Much of our own armchair philosophizing suffers in the asking of questions too vague, too broad, too inclusive. As the trial attorney knows so well, the precisely formulated question is one of the keenest tools of inquiry available to man. As the material of the last chapter indicated, it does not suffice to ask "How does this political system function?" That question in reality masks a congeries of questions, and it lacks the precision of analytical terms and concepts. It must be broken into manageable components and tackled piecemeal. Similarly, one cannot really answer a tentlike philosophical question such as "What is the best form of government?" or "Is democracy superior to all other political forms?" Each of these is a multitude of questions, and each demands many investigations and many specific answers.

In the first place, what do we mean by *democracy?* Any group of political scientists—whether they be specialists in political philosophy or not—would not easily agree. Some would want to define democracy simply as a decision-making process, as a way of reaching policy decisions in which the great number of adults are free to participate either directly or indirectly. Others would want to include some more substantive qualifications. Democracy must, in their argument, protect the rights of the individual or assure his social welfare or equality. Their view of democracy includes a view of the good society it must strive to attain. To simplify greatly, the dispute would be over whether democracy is solely a political "means" or process, or whether one must include in the definition some "ends" or goals it should achieve.[1]

Whatever one's definitional preferences, he cannot escape this kind of disagreement, for it pervades all of political science. Setting down a definition, however, is not merely a matter of rational logic or one's own preferences. Humpty Dumpty was only partly right in *Alice Through the Looking Glass* when he noted imperiously, "When *I* use a word, it means just what I choose it to mean—neither more nor less." The adequate definition must meet standards beyond the whims of the particular definer. It must be general enough to cover all relevant cases. In the case of democracy, the definition must reflect more than American, or even Western, democracy. The definition must also have criteria which enable us to apply it to the real world. One must be able to say specifically whether Brazil or Ghana or South Viet Nam is a democracy. Finally, the adequate definition must parallel and "lock into" related definitions. If democracy is the rule of the many, then its definition must fit in with definitions of rule by the few or rule by one. The working out of these definitional problems is accomplished by a combination of good logic and many observations of reality. At bottom any useful scholarly definition or concept must be a distillation of reality, a simplification or "boiling down" of many observations of the "is" into a few, logical categories.

Any concept or theory of democracy must, therefore, relate to the realities of society and individual behavior. The only alternative is to spin out fantasy Utopias for reconstructed mortals washed up on an untouched desert island—or, perhaps, an unused moon or planet. But democracy or any other political ideal must be possible within the limits of social reality. Gallons of academic ink and years of scholarly effort have gone into the examination of the prerequisites for the existence of democracy. Lists of those conditions have usually included a literate and educated population, a certain measure of economic

---

[1] For a clarification of the semantics of politics, see T. D. Weldon, *The Vocabulary of Politics* (Baltimore: Penguin Books, Inc., 1953).

security or a certain minimum standard of living, widespread popular attitudes and values supporting self-government, some degree of social mobility, and a system of communication.[2] Most of these necessary conditions for democracy have, however, been derived deductively from the definition of democracy. Only recently have political scientists begun to examine them in empirical detail.

Bernard Berelson and his associates in their study of the 1948 election in Elmira, New York, turn to these questions after examining the making of electoral decisions in that city. They express concern that the traditional theories of democracy deal with a "typical" or ideal citizen who hardly exists in reality. The voters of Elmira do not have a sustained interest in politics, do not discuss it widely, do not participate in politics, and in general know little about political choices available to them. How, then, do democracies survive if their citizens fail to measure up to the assumptions of democracy? The authors suggest the need for reconstructing our theories of democracy to de-emphasize the importance of the participating individual citizen and to stress the nature of social conflict in the society, the stability of basic social and economic institutions, and the presence of social consensus. They even suggest, in fact, that the low interest and participation levels may contribute to the success of democracy, for

> Extreme interest goes with extreme partisanship and might culminate in rigid fanaticism that could destroy democratic processes if generalized throughout the community. Low affect toward the election—not caring much—underlies the resolution of many political problems; votes can be resolved into a two-party split instead of fragmented into many parties. . . . Low interest provides maneuvering room for political shifts necessary for a complex society in a period of rapid change.

So, by this process of testing definitions and their assumptions against reality we sharpen our definitions while we assess the status quo.[3]

Up to this point we have avoided the central issue of an evaluation and justification of democracy—what is the "good" in democracy that men believe makes it worth seeking? Here one begins to break down the value of democracy into its component parts. Democracy is good

---

2 Robert A. Dahl, in his *Preface to Democratic Theory* (Chicago: University of Chicago Press, 1956), rigorously dissects the assumptions of democracy.

3 Bernard Berelson *et al.*, *Voting* (Chicago: University of Chicago Press, 1954). The quotation is on p. 314. For another excellent survey of the philosophy of democracy, see Henry Mayo, *An Introduction to Democratic Theory* (New York: Oxford University Press, 1960).

for a number of reasons (which depend on who is drafting the list): because, for example, it enables the individual to fulfill his potential, because it produces a stable society, or because it leads to the most efficient use of social resources. In other words, any value such as democracy may be broken into means-ends statements: democracy is good because it leads to X or to Y, and X and Y may be "good" because they lead to Z. The means-ends chain can and should continue until one finally comes down to the base values on which the system rests. Then, and only then, can the philosophical analysis of the value, the "ought," begin in earnest. So, as one approaches these base values, he answers one more set of "is" questions: Do the means *really* lead to those base values? To be specific, does democracy produce the stable society? Does it lead to the maximum individual self-realization?

None of the questions we have so far asked of democracy has been concerned with the "oughts," the basic issues of value and preference. They have all been questions of logic and empirical reality which surround, hide, and disguise the nub of the "ought" problem like so many prickly leaves around the heart of an artichoke. Their presence gives the lie to the oversimple dichotomy between "is" and "ought," and they impede the examination of base values. One must first clear them away, whether it is democracy or Marxian communism he would examine. The same need for definitional clarity exists if one talks of Marxian communism. That term commonly applies to a political system, an economic system, and even to a way of life. One must ask in its case, too, what attitudes and values, what social conditions, must prevail for its existence; and we must ask on what base values communism rests. Strangely, we find that its partisans and apologists use words—*freedom, justice, equality*—similar to those used by the theorists of democracy. In that case, much of the controversy between the two forms can be reduced either to problems in definition or to means-ends questions—which of the two governmental forms will more fully and effectively achieve those ends?[4]

POLITICAL MAN AND POLITICAL VALUES

Ordinary day-to-day discourse about politics abounds with statements of value preference and normative evaluation—"We ought to reform the electoral college," "Communism is only a new form of enslavement," or "Government shouldn't fix the prices of farm com-

[4] Vernon Van Dyke, *Political Science: A Philosophical Analysis* (Palo Alto, Calif.: Stanford University Press, 1960).

modities"; and the terms of evaluation—*democracy, freedom, totalitarianism, rights, equality*—sprinkle our political discussions. Although the political scientist may be more guarded and circumspect in his analysis of value questions, he does, for better or for worse, use many of the same terms the layman uses. Our discussion of political values, therefore, at least begins with semantic simplicity.

Political values are not all of a kind, however; and exploration of their variety will suggest the ways in which they enter our thoughts and conversations. To begin, political science has for centuries had two chief sets of classificatory terms: one set to describe the distribution of political power, the other to describe the role of government. The first of these sets of categories dates back to the Greek philosophers and historians; its origin in the Greek language is apparent in terms such as *democracy, oligarchy, aristocracy, monarchy, plutocracy,* and *autocracy.* All of these terms relate to the central question, "Who governs?" In whose hands does effective political power rest? Usually political scientists build this set of definitions around an old three-part division. Democracy is that government in which effective and ultimate political power is in the hands of the many, the great proportion of adults. Oligarchy is that form in which such political power rests in the hands of a comparative few. In autocracy it rests in the hands of a single person.

Within each of these categories, of course, many variations exist. Some democracies have achieved virtually complete and full adult participation, while in others large groups may be disenfranchised because of race, sex, poverty, or ethnic origin. In other cases, the formal right to participate exists, but it is an empty formality because real choice is so sharply limited. The identification of democracy in these cases, then, becomes an empirical question of identifying the locus of genuine political power in the system. As for oligarchy, the political vocabulary has a number of refined subcategories of oligarchy: plutocracy, for example, is rule by the wealthy few; aristocracy, rule by the titled or landed few; and theocracy, rule by the priestly or pious few. The definition of autocracy—or dictatorship, as we more commonly call it—is self-explanatory, although one may wonder in these days of complex, enormous political systems whether autocracy is actually a possibility in modern industrial societies. Even a self-proclaimed autarch like Adolf Hitler shared political power with party chieftains and personal confidants.

In speaking of these forms of government it should be clear that it is the political system alone of which we are talking. The categories above describe the distribution of effective *political* power, the ability to make or influence the making of the authoritative political decisions. Other terms describe the distribution of *economic* power, and intellectual anarchy results from combining or confusing the two sets of definitions. *Capitalism* refers to control of resources and means of production (i.e., economic power) by private owners and investors, *socialism* to the control of economic power by the political institutions. They are not kinds of political systems, and to confuse them with political forms is to lapse into the Marxian assumption that economic power *is* political power. There is no empirical evidence that political power is only a secondary form of economic power in all political systems, nor is there any reason to believe that any one economic system is inevitably linked with any single form of political system. Capitalism flourishes in the American democracy, but it also survived in Nazi Germany; and socialism is mixed into the economies of France, Britain, and Sweden in addition to dominating the Soviet economy.[5]

In addition to these descriptions of the distribution of political power, a second set of concepts describes the scope or role of government. These terms are addressed to the question of what government "should do" rather than to questions of "who governs." On the one hand we refer to "limited" government in which the activities of government are circumscribed and in which some areas of life are closed to its interventions. When a constitution performs these limiting tasks—and especially when it defines areas of individual freedom against government action—we use the alternative term *constitutionalism*. At the other extreme we find totalitarianism, so named because in it the concerns and functions of government are total. No aspects of life—not even family relations, religious beliefs, or the individual's livelihood—are free from the scrutiny and control of the political system.

These definitions, like all of our others, are inevitably somewhat arbitrary and imprecise. Probably in a precise sense no political system is "total," if only because the administrative and enforcement problem would be too great. Practicality, if not principle, protects the individual. Also, within the broad range of limited government there are numerous gradations. In contemporary American politics, liberals and conservatives—whatever the earlier historical meanings of those terms —disagree over the role of government. Liberals generally are more willing than conservatives for government to undertake the solution of public problems. They see government as a possible promoter and

---

[5] Robert A. Dahl, *Modern Political Analysis* (Englewood Cliffs, N.J.: Prentice-Hall, Inc., 1963).

protector of the good life, whereas conservatives fear its incursions into the choices of individuals. At the risk of oversimplification one may say that the liberals fear the power of individuals and private groups in the society, whereas conservatives fear the organized power of the political system. So, although both camps subscribe to limited government, it would be fair to say that the conservatives have opted for a more limited government than have the liberals. Furthermore, they may differ on whether specific areas of life are to be closed to government intervention. In the specific context of contemporary American politics it would be accurate to say that the position of the two ideologies would be reversed on the questions of government control of corporate power and trade-union power.

Definitions such as these may, of course, be used purely for classificatory purposes. One need never raise value questions about them; but for most individuals alive to their times and to alternative ways of life, they come to be deeply value-laden terms. They describe political preferences to which men may be emotionally attached. Beneath these general preferences, however, as we have already argued, lie base values; and these are the most difficult concepts of all to define and refine and on which to get any sort of consensus. One might take *equality,* for instance. For some it means social and economic equality as well as political equality. For others it means only the general political equality of "one man, one vote." For still others it refers to some vague equality of opportunity to seek effective political or social or economic equality. The problem persists with a concept of justice. Plato's definition of justice in the *Republic* (the giving of every man his due according to his role and status in life) would win few supporters among thoughtful democrats today. Yet consensus on an alternative is not easily achieved. Nor does agreement prevail about *freedom.* There is a vast difference between the "freedoms" of speech, press, association, and religion of the first amendment to the Constitution of the United States and the frequently quoted freedoms from want and fear formulated by Franklin Roosevelt.

It might be well to stop here and take philosophical stock for a minute. Conflict on basic vocabulary between democracy and Soviet communism, or between American liberalism and conservatism, is not great. Certain words in the international political vocabulary— words such as *democracy, freedom, justice,* and *equality*—are so potent, so loaded with favorable connotation, that no side will abandon them. They are standards to which everyone repairs; hence, one has to look beneath them for real differences. For example, one hears both liberals and conservatives in the United States argue that their philosophies will promote individual freedom. The nub of the matter, of course, is in that elusive word *freedom*. For the conservative it is much more likely to include economic freedom and the rights of property; the liberals' concept of freedom is more likely to emphasize civil and political rights. They differ, too, over whether or not government is the greatest enemy of personal freedom. Only when we give the concept of freedom some specific meaning do we see clearly the conflict of political values. The task here, as always, is to give the concept meaning in terms of real choices and possibilities in a real political system in the real world.

We have talked thus far of two main categories of political values which enter both popular and scholarly discourse: those concerned with the forms of government (both those concerned with the distribution of political power and those defining the scope of government) and those expressing basic political preferences, such as freedom and equality. We now turn to two more types: institutional preferences and policy goals.

Political institutions are means to ends, but we come to value them as desirable ends in themselves—often losing sight of the end values they were designed to promote. We argue in the United States over the performance of the Congress; its critics charge it is unresponsive, inefficient, and run by a self-selected elite. Scholars, for their part, have often charged that the American political parties fail to govern, that they fail to discipline the men they elect to office on their label and platform. Large numbers of thoughtful Americans have their pet schemes for reforming what they believe to be an archaic electoral college. Political scientists have also long been fascinated by the relative merits of cabinet-parliamentary government compared with the American separation of powers, and good-government groups all over the United States support the inauguration of city-manager government; but what goals have the existing arrangements failed to meet? Do we tamper with political institutions for aesthetic reasons; do we rearrange them, like so much furniture in the living room, for the sake of novelty and a "new look?"

Ultimately the justifications for institutional preferences fall into two categories: they promote a particular distribution of political power and/or they help reach certain basic political values. Criticism of the Congress—and especially its committees and "establishment"—as "unresponsive" is largely an argument that these institutions promote a distribution of power that excludes or minimizes the influence of certain groups (in this case, liberal and reform groups). Often the two forms of justification are wrapped together in a single cause.

Attacks on the Supreme Court's recent use of its power to interpret the constitution have been inspired both by those who object to its support of the political power of certain groups (e.g., the Negro, minorities, the political dissident) and also by those who fear that its actions undermine either institutional values (such as the separation of powers or popular democracy itself) or some base value such as economic freedom or the security of society. Since men tend to find high-minded philosophical reasons for their opinions, the preference-justification of the first kind (the promotion of a certain power distribution) is often rationalized in terms of broader, more abstract, selfless political or institutional values. So, debate over the apportionment of state legislatures goes on at both levels—as a clash over the distribution of urban and rural political power and also as a dialogue about alternative theories of democratic representation.

Particular institutional arrangements often receive another kind of justification—that of the well-being of the system itself. Scholars made a persuasive case, after observing the fall of a Cabinet about every eight months in Fourth Republic France, that this sort of political instability (and the institutions that contributed to it) was undesirable simply because it impeded the operation of the political system. Of such functional (or "systemic") values, two points should be noted. First, we often underestimate the flexibility of the system itself. Contrary to the prophecies of political Cassandras, the American federal system has adapted to the shift of power from state to nation. No American institutions, in fact, have had to be preserved in their pristine eighteenth-century state to maintain the healthy operation of the American political system. Furthermore, we may perceive false functional values. Much of the argument for independent commissions and city managers hinges on their "efficiency"; but government is not an economic organization, and its operation and functioning is not judged by the ledger or balance sheet. Efficiency is *a* value, but not one which defines the well-being of the system. The political leadership and responsiveness of a mayor-council system may be goals more important than the sheer financial efficiency of the manager plan. It was, after all, in Mussolini's Italy that government prided itself on putting the railroad trains back on schedule.

Finally, we bring all of these values and others to debates over public policy. There they become policy values—goals which we want government to recognize and enforce through the authoritative policy it makes. A searing debate over a civil-rights act raises questions of the very nature of democracy and limited government, of base values such as freedom and equality, of institutional values such as federalism and states' rights. The question of farm price supports suggests a similar range of value considerations: the proper role of government in the economy, the responsibility of a democracy for the economic well-being of its citizens, and the optimum balance of urban and rural political influence. Furthermore, both of these policy questions suggest means-ends problems. Is the civil-rights act or the farm-price-support bill the most effective way of achieving its policy values?

All manner of otherwise nonpolitical values also enter into policy questions and become policy goals. In the case of the farm price supports, the whole range of economic and social values intrudes, from the nature of free enterprise in agriculture to the social value of the family farm. In other policy debates moral values may enter. They abound in issues of legalized gambling, control of alcoholic beverages, and aid to unmarried mothers. In fact, wide-ranging government of this century touches in some way virtually all the values men hold important.

So great is the welter of policy goals, so seemingly hopeless is the resolution of their conflict, that men have long sought a higher, a first, policy goal: the "public interest." Yet it appears to be no real solution. Despite its semantic euphony, and perhaps because of it, the "public interest" means virtually all things to all men; and more importantly, its meaning takes the form of one of the kinds of values we have already discussed. For some citizens and political scientists the public interest is a shorthand for the value of democracy and its subsidiary values. For others it is the achievement of base values such as freedom or the security of the political system. There are also those who see in it the support of majority interests or some particular distribution of political power (e.g., a greater attention to the interests of consumers). Some justify it in terms of policy goals—the maintenance of an unregulated free-enterprise capitalism, for instance—or in terms of the value of the healthy working of the political system itself; but it has no autonomous meaning of its own, no magic incantatory power to pull us above the clash of policy goals, no matter how many times we utter it. There is, unhappily for those weary of indecision and conflict, no easy substitute for the difficult balancing of conflicting goals and values in the making of public policy. That process of compromise and accommodation—followed by acceptance—lies close to the nature of stability in a political system.[6]

---

[6] Carl J. Friedrich (ed.), *The Public Interest* (New York: Atherton Press, 1962).

THE JUSTIFICATION OF VALUES

After one has identified political values and observed how they enter political debate, the troublesome problem of final justification remains. Is there no way of saying "These goals are good," or "These political arrangements are preferable to those?" Have we no fixed standards, no philosophical measuring sticks, by which we can assess various ways of governing? On this most fundamental question in political philosophy political scientists—and all scholars, for that matter—are divided.

Those scholars who believe we *have* the measuring stick are frequently called "philosophical absolutists." That is to say, they believe that there exist universal, fixed, and unchanging standards of good and truth, and that political systems can and must be built on them. Their conviction, of course, extends beyond politics; for if there are fixed and immutable values for the political system, there must also be those for social and personal life. These values, as I have argued, cannot be proved empirically. Social scientists cannot apply their methods of observing reality to prove the validity of Thomas Jefferson's affirmation that all men "are endowed by their creator with certain unalienable rights; that among these are life, liberty, and the pursuit of happiness. . . . " No amount of data or analysis will establish the validity or superiority of Jefferson's values over those of philosophies of the divine and absolute rights of monarchs which were so common in his day.

If not by empirical methods, how does one establish, validate, or "prove" his absolute values? The most enduring and influential approach among the philosophical absolutists of the Western world has been that of the natural law. From the ancient Greek Stoics, through John Locke and the American founding fathers, and down to contemporary writers such as Jacques Maritain, men have believed that there are in the very nature of man and society certain natural laws of social and moral relationship. Since they inhere in the very nature of man and creation, they have ultimate roots in the will of the Creator. They are, again in Jefferson's phrase, the law of "nature and of nature's God." That a man's life is sacred and that one man must not murder another is rooted in the very humanness of man and in the necessities of society. Murder violates both the fundamental nature of man, his humanness, and the mission of society. Just as physical laws such as those of gravity bind the physical world together and enable it to "work," so these natural laws join men and groups together in harmonious relationships; and from these natural laws one furthermore deduces a series of "natural rights" of the individual—the rights of life, liberty, and the pursuit of happiness, for example.

How does one discover or determine these natural laws? Or for that matter, how does one discover *any* set of absolute values? One perceives the natural law by a classical humanistic, rational, common-sense knowledge of man—by the kind of intuitive knowledge of man and society which any serious, educated, rigorous intellect is capable of. It can, indeed, be known and grasped and appreciated by any rational man. These natural laws, these "truths," said Jefferson, are "self-evident." They are in the nature of things and can be seen by people attuned to natural "essences" and the basic purposes of life.[7]

So, at least, say the advocates of natural law. Many "hard-shelled" empiricists are less sanguine that such a kind of knowledge can and does exist. It is, in any event, outside of their conviction that if an event or relationship cannot be observed and verified by sense perception it is "preference" (or its rationalization) rather than knowledge. They would point out, too, that what has seemed natural has shifted from place to place, from time to time, and from observer to observer. Usury was thought by most medieval natural lawyers to violate the natural law; but today men who seem moral and respectable erect great financial empires, and even great economies, on the extension of credit and the lending of money for profit.

Although the school of natural law is the most influential representative of philosophical absolutism in the Western world, it has not been the only one. Plato, in the *Republic* and his other works, posits, too, a different but related world of "natural" truth inherent in the very essence and nature of things. Yet Plato proposes a government of a few "philosopher kings" who are to rule over the great masses of men and determine what is good for them. Also, in the fascist dictatorships of Germany and Italy philosophers and leaders claimed to see their dictatorial apparatuses, rather than the judgment of majorities, as the discoverers and bearers of final truth and of the true goals of their people. The results of these philosophical absolutisms are clearly quite different from the democracy and individualism that emerge from Jefferson's natural law. How is it that one philosophical absolutism can lead to consequences so different from those of another?[8]

---

[7] An excellent recent statement of the natural-law position is Jacques Maritain, *Man and the State* (Chicago: University of Chicago Press, 1951).

[8] Plato, *Republic*.

The essential difference between the natural-law school and those which have led to nondemocratic regimes seems to rest in a missing premise about who in society is capable of perceiving and knowing the final, absolute truth. In contrasting the positions of Plato and of John Hallowell, a contemporary American political scientist and representative of natural-law doctrines, Thomas L. Thorson carries the argument through the next step:

> Let us therefore supply the additional premises and see what happens. If for Plato's argument we add the premise "this reality which is good can only be known by a capable and highly trained few," the notion of deduction begins to make more sense. The same holds true for Hallowell if we add a different premise, namely, "this reality which is good can be known by all men." The difference between these two premises is the key to the difference between Plato's authoritarian proposal and Hallowell's democratic one.[9]

Thus, over this issue philosophic absolutism is revealed as a two-edged sword. It cuts one way with the addition of a basic premise and the other way with its alteration. Which of the two premises is correct? On that issue we are pushed back to a matter of "faith" or of the posited assumptions of a philosophic system.

Philosophic absolutism, however, is not today a popular position among empirical social scientists. They are, by and large, philosophic "relativists." Their system of knowledge tends to reject the possibility of fixed unchanging values. Values, they believe, are socially determined and validated only by their social usefulness. They grow logically out of conventional social relationships and ways of life. They vary from culture to culture, from society to society; they can be understood only in terms of the needs and the cultural assumptions of a particular society. Polygamy may be unacceptable in Western societies, but it is quite acceptable in some societies where the dangers of continual war and hazardous food-gathering deplete the male population. Indeed, the combination of the "is"-oriented empiricism of modern social science and the comparisons of cultural anthropology have put moral and ethical absolutism of any kind on the defensive in this scholarly world.[10]

---

[9] *The Logic of Democracy* (New York: Holt, Rinehart & Winston, Inc., 1962), p. 47. John Hallowell's work is best represented by *The Moral Foundation of Democracy* (Chicago: University of Chicago Press, 1954).

[10] The relativist position is well stated by Arnold Brecht, *Political Theory: The Foundations of Twentieth Century Political Thought* (Princeton, N.J.: Princeton University Press, 1959).

Can the philosophical relativist, then, offer no guideposts, no standards for political judgment at all? His basic commitment to theories of knowledge and ethics precludes his saying that there are absolute, fixed values the truth of which transcends the limits of time and place. Yet, he is not willing to concede that values are unimportant or that "anything goes." To say that values are relative is not to say they do not exist. The relativist will readily concede their importance and meaning for the life of any society.

One philosophical solution for the philosophical relativist as he faces the question of justifying ultimate values is to hedge a bit and make just one fundamental value assumption. From it other values can be deduced and derived. Usually in democratic philosophy this assumption has proclaimed the central value of the individual. The Utilitarians, for example, posited "the greatest good for the greatest number" as their value touchstone, and others have built on the value of the maximum freedom and self-realization of the individual. From that central imperative one can begin to give meaning to basic values such as equality and to devise political institutions in harmony with them. The chief problem here, however, is the vagueness of the central commitment, for a single central value rarely contains sufficient philosophical building material out of which to erect an edifice of values. What, to be specific, does the "greatest good for the greatest number" mean? Few would want to say it means that the wishes of the majority are automatically good and true. It must, in other words, mean more than sheer majoritarianism. But if so, what must it mean? And how does one measure the "greatest good"? And since we are trying to define *the good,* don't we beg the question if our answer also is couched in terms of *good?*

The other alternative for the relativist is to work within a fixed set of values. The political philosopher may well say that a particular society has a traditional, fixed set of value commitments that one merely has to accept as a "given." Within that value context the job of the philosopher is to clarify subsidiary political values and make sure they are congruent with the more fundamental values and traditions of the society. If the dominant values are those of the Judeo-Christian heritage, in other words, he works within their context. The question of whether these are fixed and eternal values need never come up. It is enough that large numbers of people—probably including the philosopher himself—approve of them and at least try to act on them. It is his task in such a society to develop basic concepts of freedom and political responsibility which are compatible with its heritage. The way he balances the unending tension between the aspirations of the individual for freedom and the needs of society for stability and security will be shaped by the commitments of the heritage.[11]

Perhaps the answer of the philosophical relativist to the question of ultimate justification has to be, "Sorry, you're asking me the wrong question. The search for unchanging values is philosophically futile. Since these value commitments are fairly firmly fixed in any society, it's also futile in practical terms." The American Pragmatists have probably faced up to the analysis of political values most candidly and directly. They grant the relativity of values and argue that the job of philosophy is to re-examine values constantly in the light of the effect they have on the real world. That effect, of course, can be observed empirically. In this sense philosophical "truth" is determined by the results and outcome of values. That constant examination of the consequences of values enables us, therefore, to reshape and readjust values to new social demands and problems. It can also tell us whether we are achieving our values, or whether perhaps our means are missing the mark or actually reshaping the ends they purport to achieve.

Apart from their differences on the justification of basic values, the philosophical absolutists and relativists share a common burden in evaluating the political system. They can clarify and define the values of the system, pointing to logical inconsistencies where necessary; they can devise practical political arrangements for achieving great ends; they can study the roots and reasons for traditional values and value heritages; and they can point out how and with what effect our values shape our political behavior. Conversely, they can suggest as well how our behavior shapes our values, how, for instance, we alter basic values of law by resorting to private violence and vigilantism.

Above all, their concern for a rigorous philosophical analysis, as we have seen in this chapter, unites the empirical and philosophical traditions within political science; for analysis of the "is" is vital to the understanding of norms and values, and the ideal framework of the "ought" gives social meaning and utility to our study of the "is." In their interdependence is the basic unity of the study of politics.

---

11 This position is, I think, close to that of Thorson's excellent analysis.

Suggested Methods for Teachers

chapter six

Raymond H. Muessig
Vincent R. Rogers

> For we are the only people who think him that
> does not meddle in state affairs not indolent,
> but good for nothing.
>
> PERICLES

The word *idiot* is derived from the Greek *idiotes*, which meant "those citizens who do not take part in public voting." Although in ancient Greece the *idiotes* failed to vote because they were not *permitted* to and although the word has taken on a different meaning today, when one considers the large number of Americans who *choose* not to participate in local, state, and national elections, the word (with its twentieth-century connotation) may not after all be an entirely inappropriate political adjective.

Many political scientists, however, would shy away from such value-laden pronouncements. They are interested, of course, in *who* votes and who does not. They gather data about voters' religious affiliation, socio-economic status, educational background, and so forth. They are *not* usually prepared to say (in any scholarly or academic capacity) that the nonvoter is or is not an "idiot," lazy, or irresponsible. A number of political scientists are generally content with describing what is, and they leave it to others to decide whether or not things are "good" or "bad."

This attitude may be appropriate for some practicing political scientists. Yet it presents certain problems for those of us who are concerned with the education of children in the United States. It is

75

important that American youth emerge from their schooling with solid understandings of and attachments to democratic tenets, processes, and procedures as a way of adult political life. Education for young people in a democracy *is* different from education for children and youth in a totalitarian state. Our attempts to translate Dr. Sorauf's ideas into an action program for schools and teachers must include some attention to questions having to do with American ideals, commitments, and loyalties.

On the other hand, there is a great deal more to political science than the inculcation of values, as Dr. Sorauf has so carefully and vividly pointed out. This chapter will not, therefore, be given over completely to "citizenship education," although this area does have a place as a concern in social studies education in general and in a publication such as this one. Neither will the chapter emphasize student government and a host of other possible citizenship projects.

Rather, it will attempt to help the classroom teacher illustrate in his everyday teaching broad and significant concepts and generalizations drawn from political science. We have tried to emphasize selected ideas that seem to be of particular significance to political scientists *but* also seem to offer fruitful possibilities for classroom teachers in a democratic society. We have not attempted to deal with *all* of the topics that might be taught in elementary or secondary schools that are in some way related to political science.

We hope that the ideas suggested here will stimulate teachers to develop new methods of their own, to read more deeply, to probe, to experiment. We expect the teacher to adapt our suggestions to his own situation rather than to use them "as is," regardless of the needs, interests, abilities, and aspirations of his students.

Finally, we wish to make it clear that neither Dr. Sorauf nor we have put forth a "program" or new curriculum in political science. We do see a place for political science in the schools, however; and we wish to encourage among classroom teachers a more mature and meaningful approach to that discipline.

As a minimum condition for its existence a society establishes authoritative institutions that can make decisions which are binding on all the people, provide for the resolution of dissent, and effectively enforce basic rules.

The nature and organization of common social studies curricula in many American elementary and secondary schools provides an almost limitless number of opportunities to develop, clarify, and reinforce this basic understanding. For example, in the primary grades children are exposed frequently to units dealing with school, family, and neighborhood. Perceptive teachers of young children should recognize easily the parallel between the decision-making and -enforcing functions of these institutions and the activities of more formal, pervasive state and federal governmental agencies. The fire drill is an obvious example of a requirement that is binding on all members of the school society, and youngsters can see the necessity for certain behavior and its prompt enforcement when the alarm sounds. Disagreements between pupils must often be resolved by the classroom teacher when other means have failed. The relationship between a group of rules and some of their consonant reasons should be perceived by children as they consider such matters as school-bus procedures, the use of student patrolmen at selected crosswalks, the sectioning of the playground for various kinds of activity, and so on. The child's first experiences in school can be used, then, as a vehicle for exploring and discussing the types of rules necessary to make his classroom and his school run more effectively and safely, and even more pleasantly.

Some primary teachers find that Jerrold Beim's *The Taming of Toby* [1] is useful in approaching an idea such as the political science generalization we have identified above. The story is about a boy who tends to ignore rules and do as he pleases without regard to how his actions affect others. He is inconsiderate, ignores the rights of others, and even harms some children physically. Perhaps the children might attempt to write a class or group story about a mythical school in which Toby's behavior would be "normal." The children might act out portions of a "typical day" in the imaginary school or simply suggest as many things as possible which could occur in such a setting. Eventually, the teacher might invite a discussion of questions like this one:

What might happen if everyone in our class were to go home whenever he wanted, take a walk outdoors or go down the hall to visit a brother or sister, or take things that did not belong to him?

Children in their early school years could be encouraged to follow up a discussion like this by searching for additional illustrations drawn from society at large. They might suggest some of the possible conse-

---

[1] New York: William Morrow & Co., Inc., 1953.

quences of the violation of traffic laws by adult motorists, the failure to adhere to fundamental sanitation standards, the refusal to pay various bills at the end of the month, and so forth. A further understanding that could be introduced at the primary level is that rules, regulations, and laws may have different areas and levels of applicability and degrees of enforcement. A rule may apply to one person but not another in the same environment. A regulation may affect one individual because he is in a particular situation with unique responsibilities but not another individual functioning in a different setting involving other expectations. A law may be operational only locally, or it may be in effect at state, national, or even international levels.

With young children, the teacher could discuss a fictitious family in which rules have been established about eating all of the food on the plate at each meal, having candy only after dinner, brushing teeth after eating, changing into play clothes after school, going to bed at a certain time, and so on. The children might be asked to list the family members subject to these rules. The class would probably point out that the baby has a bottle instead of a plate and stops drinking when he is full, has no teeth to brush, and sleeps whenever he wants to. It might be observed that the parents go to bed at a later hour, and so on. Then the children could be shown pictures of other hypothetical families and asked to tell what effect the *first* family's rules would have on *them*. The teacher might also inquire whether the person or persons who usually enforce rules in one family do the same thing for all of the other families in a given neighborhood. The idea being developed here could be further expanded by a discussion of whether all rules would be identical from school to school and whether regulations enforced by one city would be applicable to another city hundreds of miles away. Children can see easily that rules regarding cafeteria serving times and lines would be applicable in one school with a cafeteria but not in a second school where children eat sack lunches in their classrooms. They may have observed parking signs, meters, and law-enforcement officers in a large downtown section of a city and the absence of all of these things in a little suburban area or a rural town. They should be able to grasp why some states have a number of rigidly enforced laws to protect forests and wildlife whereas this is not so important a concern in a few others, and they should gradually uncover some laws that apply to *every* American.

The class might summarize its ideas under headings like "Things Each Family Decides for Itself," "Things Each School Decides for

Itself," and "Laws *Everyone* Must Obey." Eventually, then, children should be able to perceive that rules, regulations, and laws touch the lives of people in many ways and that school rules apply to *everyone* attending the school, city regulations pertain to *everyone* living in a given city, state laws affect *everyone* residing in a particular state, and national laws are binding upon *everyone* falling under a specific nation's jurisdiction.

Virginia Sorensen's moving children's story *Plain Girl* provides teachers in the intermediate grades with a number of illustrations of the pervasiveness of certain kinds of laws in our society. The story concerns Esther Lapp, a ten-year-old Amish girl who lives on a farm in Pennsylvania. In this excerpt, two officials of the state government have just arrived:

. . . An automobile stood by the front gate. Two strange men without any hats on their heads at all, or any beards on their chins, sat in the seat, looking toward the house. She hurried inside with the hens and closed the door quickly behind her. But she went at once to the wired opening across the front and looked out.

It was a shining black car with a colored picture painted on the door. There were words too, but she could not read them so far away. . . .

The barn door opened. Father came out. On Father anger showed very plainly because it almost never happened to him. Now his beard looked so stiff and fierce that he did not seem like Father at all. . . .

. . . [The men] climbed out of the car and came through the gate and straight toward where Father stood. The first man carried a paper in one hand, reading as he walked. When he came close to Father, he looked up and said, "I understand you have a daughter, Esther Lapp?"

Esther jumped from the window so quickly that the chickens at her feet flew in every direction, squawking. Then she stood still, against the door.

"Yes," she heard Father say. "I have a daughter Esther."

.   .   .   .

"From our records, we find that she is almost ten years old," the man said. . . . "Why hasn't she ever been to school?"

.   .   .   .

"We have taught Esther here at home," [Father] said. "She is able to read and write very well now. In English. And in German too."

"That may be so," the man said, and glanced at his companion. "But it happens, Mr. Lapp, that we have a compulsory school law in Pennsylvania. I'm sure you remember—we have talked about this matter before."

"Quite some time ago now," said the other man. "Before, I believe, the trouble was about your son." He looked at the paper in his companion's hand. "Our records show that you were arrested and fined three times before he finally went to school. Daniel Lapp. Isn't that your son?"

Father did not answer, and Esther began to tremble from her head to her toes. . . .

. . . "You finally sent Daniel to school, and he finished," the man said. "We understood you meant to send your daughter without trouble when the time came."

"Esther is learning here at home," Father said slowly in a heavy stubborn voice. "We Amish people believe in the law; you should know it. But we do not believe in a bad law that forces men to send their children to learn bad ways. We are able to teach our children everything they will need to know here on the farm."

.   .   .   .

"Believe me, Mr. Lapp, we're sorry about this," the first man said. "But until you people provide a good school of your own—one the Superintendent can approve, mind you—every Amish child must go to the school provided. . . .

.   .   .   .

. . . "We are to inform you, Mr. Lapp, that your daughter Esther must be in school from the age of eight until she is seventeen. Her case has been overlooked too long already."

.   .   .   .

"On September the 8th, next week," [the other man] said, "the school bus will come along this road. If your daughter does not appear, Mr. Lapp, you will be arrested before night."

.   .   .   .

[The two men] got into the car again. To turn it around they had to drive it into the yard and back it up. Esther could see the picture quite clearly for a minute, a blue design like a shield. She could read the words too: THE COMMONWEALTH OF PENNSYLVANIA.[2]

After the teacher has read the preceding passage and provided some background information about the Amish people, he might ask his class questions similar to these:

Do you think Esther's father should have been forced to send her to school? Why or why not?

Since Esther's father did not like the law, was it right to *make* him obey it? Why or why not?

Why do laws such as this exist?

Do you think that it is important for everyone to go to school? Why or why not?

---

[2] Abridged from *Plain Girl*, © 1955, by Virginia Sorensen. Reprinted by permission of Harcourt, Brace & World, Inc.

What might our state be like if there were no such law?

What kinds of rules *can* Esther's family make?

The class might conclude this discussion by listing *other* rules, regulations, and laws that come from outside the family and that must be obeyed by all.

Many children learn quite early in life that the President of the United States is the most important leader in their country, and perhaps a number of youngsters see the chief executive as a sort of benevolent authority figure. Frequently, children lack actual knowledge of the President's functions, the schedule he keeps, the difficulties he encounters daily, and the weighty decisions he has to make. Although there are biographical materials that teachers might use to enlarge children's understandings of the Presidency, Herbert Hoover's little volume, *On Growing Up,* provides some of the most appealing, readable, direct answers to children's questions. The following is an example of an eighth-grader's letter to the former President and his personal reply:

Dear Mr. Hoover:

I am in the eighth grade and am writing a term-paper on the Executive Branch of the United States Government. I would very much like to have your views and opinions on the following questions:

1. What part of the President's job would you consider the hardest? Why?

2. In what ways, if any, do you feel that the President's responsibilities are being added on to his already heavy load?

I would very much appreciate your reply.

Thank-you

Very Much!!

Yours Truly,

SUSAN ———

My dear Susan:

You ask: "What part of the President's job would you consider the hardest?"

The answer is: Making a dozen decisions a day.

You also ask: "In what ways, if any, do you feel that the President's responsibilities are being added on to his already heavy load?"

The answer is: The Communists add to his burdens every minute of the twenty-four hours.[3]

---

[3] Herbert Hoover, *On Growing Up* (New York: William Morrow & Co., Inc., 1962), pp. 58–59. Copyright © 1949, 1959, 1962, by Herbert Hoover. All rights reserved.

Material of this sort might easily lead to a discussion of the *kinds* of decisions a President must make. The class could divide a bulletin board into two sections—one labeled "Foreign" and the other "Domestic." As a continuing current-events activity, examples of the Presidential exercise of authority as revealed in daily newspapers would be brought into class, categorized, posted, and discussed. Gradually, the class might develop a group of subheadings dealing with kinds of decisions such as "Financial," "Military," and others.

As older students dig into the exploration and settlement of America, they might give particular attention to some of the "political" problems of the early settlers. They could be asked to role-play a situation such as the following:

Pretend you have just dropped anchor off the coast of America. The year is 1620. There are around a hundred people in your party who are planning on settling permanently in this new land. Before anyone starts to go ashore, a group of the older men on board who helped organize the expedition sit down together. They want to discuss the problems of living together in this unsettled wilderness. One of the men speaks. . . .

Undoubtedly the class will deal with questions relating to food, shelter, sickness, and Indians. Gradually, however, the teacher should push them to look past the problems of immediate survival and to consider fundamental issues involved in forming a new society. Later, the *Mayflower Compact* might be discussed as an example of the steps taken by real people who arrived in the New World at this time. Students might consider also what would have happened if *no* rules were formulated; if each family went off on its own; if there were no leaders who had the authority to make vital decisions; if there were no way to enforce basic rules.

High-school students might gain some perspective from reading Golding's *Lord of the Flies*. This stimulating, often frightening novel explores the behavior of a group of boys marooned on an island without any adult authority—without "official" rules, regulations, or laws of any kind. Initially, the boys run their own affairs as they might have done back home. They choose a sensible, humane leader; attempt to build shelters; light a huge signal fire to attract passing ships; hold meetings and run them in a relatively democratic way. In time, however, the discipline represented and required by Ralph, their elected leader, is resented by the rest of the boys. Their European-oriented "society of law" begins to break down, and a different society emerges. The passage below describes the transition; another boy, Jack, has challenged Ralph's leadership:

> ". . . Who are you, anyway? Sitting there telling people what to do. You can't hunt, you can't sing—"
> "I'm chief. I was chosen."
> "Why should choosing make any difference? Just giving orders that don't make any sense—"
>
> .   .   .   .
>
> "Jack!"
> Jack's voice sounded in bitter mimicry.
> "Jack! Jack!"
> "The rules!" shouted Ralph. "You're breaking the rules!"
> "Who cares?"
> Ralph summoned his wits.
> "Because the rules are the only thing we've got!"
> But Jack was shouting against him.
> "Bollocks to the rules! We're strong—we hunt! If there's a beast, we'll hunt it down! We'll close in and beat and beat and beat—!"
> He gave a wild whoop and leapt down to the pale sand. At once the platform was full of noise and excitement, scramblings, screams and laughter. The assembly shredded away and became a discursive and random scatter from the palms to the water and away along the beach, beyond night-sight. . . .[4]

At this point, the class might exchange opinions on whether or not the aggregate of boys could still be called a society. The students could be stimulated to define *society* in their own terms first and then to consult a dictionary. Next, they might be provided with a group of political science sources and encouraged to analyze definitions of *society* found there. They could also suggest some hypotheses about the *future* of the group of boys. What may happen if the boys continue to react in the manner described in the excerpt read aloud in class? Are the boys likely to continue in this fashion? If not, what kind of system of authority and regulation of behavior seems most likely to develop?

High-school students might investigate a number of situations in which societal rules, regulations, and laws have been openly defied. One of the most dramatic, moving, and thought-provoking illustrations of disregard for constituted authority appears in William Van Tilburg

---

[4] William Golding, *Lord of the Flies* (New York: Coward-McCann, Inc.). Copyright © 1954 by William Gerald Golding.

Clark's *The Ox-Bow Incident.*[5] This story of the West is tautly written and quickly paced. It deals with the hanging of three innocent men by a posse which will not take the time to gather and carefully examine and verify evidence and go through normal legal procedures. Students might discuss the implications of defiance of the law, both to the individual and to society as a whole. They might respond to a question dealing with whether a society can survive in anything resembling its present form if disregard for all legally constituted authority becomes prevalent.

Students at the high-school level could also reflect on the social, legal, and moral problems inherent in the disregard of societal standards evident in contemporary incidents related to civil rights. The case of a Georgia restaurant-owner who defied the Civil Rights Act of 1964 by refusing to serve Negroes, an account of white mothers blocking the integration of a Southern school, the defiant statements made by the governors of Alabama and Mississippi, and the reports of the riots that have occurred in the Negro sections of Northern cities could be discussed. Questions such as the following might be considered:

What is the role of the Southern citizen who is convinced that integration is wrong?

How can he protest *within* the framework of the law and the value system of his society at large?

What avenues are open to Northern Negroes who are discriminated against as they seek jobs and housing?

What might happen if disregard for the law of the land becomes more prevalent?

The larger a society is, the more an individual must rely upon group membership and representation to achieve his aims. By uniting with others he is able to increase the strength of his voice and improve the chances that his wishes will be made known to those in decision-making positions.

America is known as a nation of "joiners." People are frequently members of a large number and variety of groups, many of them purely social. Some groups are business and professional organizations; others are frankly political; and still others fall into additional categories. Population increases and technological advances have created a much larger, far more complex society than existed at our

---

[5] New York: New American Library of World Literature, Inc., 1960.

nation's inception. This society apparently requires a proportionately complex government, a government the individual citizen finds increasingly difficult to influence, affect, or shape. The individual therefore forms, joins, and supports groups designed to give his views a more articulate, broadened, amplified hearing.

Elementary-school teachers might approach the teaching of this second idea drawn from political science by using a few letters written by children to various government officials. These letters are generally filled with the innocence, optimism, and sincerity of childhood; they are often humorous, sometimes deeply moving, and on rare occasions beautifully imbued with the essential spirit of democracy. The following requests received by the late President John F. Kennedy are compelling illustrations:

Dear Mr. President,
    I would like permission to have a tractor to knock down 11 trees. The reason we want them knocked down is for a baseball field across the street from my house.
    If this is permitted we boys will be very grateful.
                                        Thank you
                                        Sincerely
                                            JAY B————6

Dear John F. Kennedy,
    I want to stop all wars but I can't because I'm too little. I'm 7½ years old. I don't like wars. I think its stupid and nobody can make me change my mind. And if you can I want you to write to me a letter and tell me what you think of wars.
                                        Your friend
                                            DAVID R————7

Although these letters were assuredly written with conviction, their effectiveness as means of influencing a major decision-maker could be questioned!

Next, as a current-events assignment, the teacher might suggest that the class devote a week to looking for news stories that illustrate a problem of some real concern to the group. The stories could be discussed and evaluated and placed on a large bulletin board. At the end of the week the children would be asked to choose any story that they all feel is important enough to do something about. Current-events time during the next few weeks might be reserved for looking for news items dealing with ways people make their

---

6 William Adler, *Kids' Letters To President Kennedy* (New York: William Morrow & Co., Inc., 1961), p. 91. Copyright © 1961, by Bill Adler. A selection of letters from this volume has appeared in *McCall's Magazine*. All rights reserved.
7 *Ibid.*, p. 150.

views known to those in government. Class members might find a story dealing with people picketing a governor's mansion, one concerned with telegrams being sent by constituents to a particular senator, one describing a group calling upon an elected representative, one telling about a petition being circulated in a given area, and so on. At this point, the class might try to develop a technique they could employ that would be relevant to the solution of the problem identified. Pupils might ask questions such as:

Where should we begin?

Should all of us work on this right away, or should we elect a committee to do some thinking about this first?

Can we do something about this problem all by ourselves, or should we try to get help from others?

Would there be some adults who care about this problem too? Would they have some ideas about what should be done?

As an adjunct to this exercise, a state legislator might be invited by the class to discuss some of the most effective and least effective ways to influence governmental changes and improvements. The resource person might mention the types of letters he receives from individual citizens and groups of voters. If it is not possible for a public servant to visit the classroom, the children might write to one or more state and national legislators about their questions.

Perhaps upper-elementary and junior-high-school students would add to their understanding of the role of the organized group in American political life by examining written descriptions of the activities of certain legislators. Donald Matthews' provocative study, *U. S. Senators and Their World*, contains a wealth of information of this kind. For example, here is a description of a more or less typical day in the life of the late Senator Richard Neuberger of Oregon:

7:45– 8:30 A.M.	Take orange juice with my wife, drive to Capitol Building.
8:30– 9:30 A.M.	Have breakfast with leader of Railroad Brotherhoods from Oregon and his wife; take them onto Senate floor and show them my desk—which is permitted only when the Senate is not in session.
9:30–10:00 A.M.	Confer with administrative assistant and other members of my staff about day's agenda, important letters and telegrams.
1:30– 2:15 P.M.	Have as guests in Senate Restaurant college coed from Oregon who is studying drama in New York

	City and her girl friend, a delegate to Young Republican meeting. (Because I was late for lunch, as usual, my wife was present to get our guests started.)
2:15– 3:15 P.M.	Attend Senate session and participate in debate on amendments to farm bill. Called off floor four times for interviews with delegations from "home" and once to be questioned by Associated Press reporter about campaign spending bills.
4:30– 5:30 P.M.	Dictate to secretary in alcove just off Marble Reading Room, answering personally more than forty letters and telegrams.
5:30– 6:30 P.M.	Return to office to sign mail and be briefed by staff about information and messages brought by steady stream of callers during day.
6:45– 7:30 P.M.	Return to Senate floor to make insertions in *Record* of several editorials from Oregon papers, prior to close of day's debate.
8:00–10:00 P.M.	Dinner at downtown Washington hotel with Oregon's Chancellor of Higher Education, in city for conferences with Veterans Administration on GI training.
12:00– 1:00 A.M.	Go to bed, discuss with wife events of day . . . the telephone can ring at any moment (during the night), and often does. I have been awakened by a constituent who wanted me to facilitate his bidding on a Defense Department contract, by an Oregon GI who ran afoul of MP's in Louisiana for alleged drunken driving, and by a female voter 3,000 miles away who wondered if my wife ". . . would be good enough to compute her income tax . . " [8]

Following the reading of this account of Senator Neuberger's day, the class might be asked to list all the ways in which "pressure" was brought to bear upon the senator. The class might divide these into "individual" and "group" sections. Having made this distinction, the students could attempt to enlarge the number of items listed under the "group" category by attempting to think beyond one representative day in a senator's life. In a brain-storming session, the class might add a large number of organizations they feel would have reason to attempt to influence a legislator. Next, a list of key bills passed in the last session of Congress could be written on the chalkboard, and

[8] Donald R. Matthews, *U. S. Senators and Their World* (Chapel Hill: University of North Carolina Press, 1960), pp. 80–81.

the class might hypothesize about the groups that would be most likely to have an interest (either pro or con) in such legislation. Or, a single bill (local *or* national in scope) could be explored in depth in terms of the groups which might be concerned with its passage or defeat. Having formulated hypotheses about the political interests and activities of certain organizations, the class might write to a few groups for specific information about their positions on the bill and about their activities, if any, directed toward its adoption or rejection. Finally, the class might return to the original listing of "individual" and "group" pressures directed toward Senator Neuberger, in an attempt to assess their possible *effects*. Specifically, students might discuss *which* attempts, individual or group, would be *most* likely to have an impact on the Senator in the long run and why this might be so.

Still another approach might involve a simple survey of the groups represented by young people in a given class and by their parents. Individual students could list on separate three-by-five cards each organization to which either they or their parents belong. All of the cards could be thrown into a container, mixed up, and then withdrawn and categorized. The organizations represented would include such groups as the Y.M.C.A., the Girl Scouts, 4-H, the First Methodist Church, the Knights of Columbus, B'nai B'rith, the Republican and Democratic parties, the Rotary Club, the League of Women Voters, the American Legion, the Izaak Walton League of America, the PTA, the Acme Garage Bowling Team, the Happy Times Square Dancing Club, the Model Railroading Club, and many, many others. The class might then discuss reasons why such groups exist, including instructional, religious, political, business, patriotic, conservational, recreational, and other purposes. An examination of such groups should lead to the observation that many groups, while not organized primarily for political reasons, do upon occasion carry out political functions. Teachers could amplify the operations of such groups by inviting representatives of a few organizations such as the PTA, the American Legion, and the Izaak Walton League to come to class and to describe activities in which they engage. In particular, the class might probe into the origins of a given group and the reasons for its founding. Students could also find out whether or not the group has a specific legislative program and, if so, how it attempts to influence governmental decision-makers.

Another approach towards a better understanding of the political role played by organized groups in a modern, complex society involves an analysis of certain election campaign procedures. Junior- and senior-high-school students might be asked to examine systematically a variety of such activities. For example, one group might read specific newspapers, looking for paid political advertisements. Another group might record similar radio and television appeals. A third group could study selected periodicals while a fourth analyzed material sent through the mail and a fifth looked for billboards. In all cases, the students would be attempting to identify and list the *groups* responsible for the advertisements, spot announcements, mailing pieces, or displays. They would be on the lookout in particular for groups such as "American Scientists for Smith," "The Hometown Taxpayer's League for Jones," and "Big City Auto-workers for Brown." Eventually, the class might focus on *why* such groups exist. To further clarify the generalization toward which this approach is directed, the class might compare the number and variety of groups acting on behalf of a presidential candidate with the organizations active in a purely local campaign. The class might even make a hypothetical comparison between the number of groups operating in an American election campaign with the political groups (if any) likely to exist in societies like those of the Papuans of New Guinea, of the Australian Aborigines, of the Eskimos of the far north, etc.

The American labor movement offers hundreds of obvious examples of the necessity for the individual to organize in order to make his wishes known not only to his employers but also to those in decision-making positions in government. Although there are many opportunities to examine the role played by organized labor through the course of American history, documents such as the one quoted below—a list of rules and regulations in a nineteenth-century American woolen mill—might be used to initiate studies of this sort.

RULES & REGULATIONS
To be Observed by All Persons
Employed in the Factory of
AMASA WHITNEY

Rule 1   The Mill will be put in operation 10 minutes before sun-rise at all seasons of the year. The gate will be shut 10 minutes past sunset from the 20th of March to the 20th of September; at 30 minutes past from the 20th of September to the 20th of March. Saturdays, at sunset.

2nd   It will be required of every person employed, that they be in the room in which they are employed, at the time mentioned above for the mill to be in operation.

3rd   Hands are not allowed to leave the factory in working hours, without the consent of their Overseer; if they do, they will be liable to have their time set off.

4th   Any one who by negligence or misconduct causes damage to
the machinery, or impedes the progress of the work, will
liable to make good the damage for the same. . . .

. . . .

9th   Any thing tending to impede the progress of manufacturing
in working hours, such as unnecessary conversation, reading,
eating fruit, & &, must be avoided. . . .

. . . .

13th   It is intended that the bell be rung 5 minutes before the gate
is hoisted, so that all persons may be ready to start their
machinery precisely at the time mentioned. . . .

. . . .

15th   . . . 25 minutes will be allowed for breakfast, 30 minutes
for dinner, and 25 minutes for supper. . . .

16th   The hands will leave the factory so that the doors may be
fastened within 10 minutes from the time of leaving off work.

AMASA WHITNEY

Winchendon. July 5, 1830 [9]

Assuming that most twentieth-century Americans would find these
working hours and other conditions something less than ideal, the
class might be asked to dramatize a situation in which a few workers
attempt to "do something" about their problem. Perhaps a man has
been seriously injured in the factory. There is no such thing as acci-
dent insurance. The workman has lost the use of his right arm. Since
he is unable to do his job, he has been fired. Three or four workers
meet to see what might be done to help their fellow employee. The
role-players should attempt to put themselves, as best they can, in
the position of workers living during the first half of the nineteenth
century. What might they do? How can they deal with a problem
like this? What avenues of redress (if any) might be open to them?
The role-players might suggest several possible procedures, and the
class should examine the probable results of each. For example, what
might happen if three of the men went to see the boss? What would
be the strengths and weaknesses of the worker's position? What was
the general attitude at this time concerning a worker's "rights"?
Suppose the same three wrote to the governor, or went to see a
senator. Could they expect conditions to be changed? Why or why
not? How might a farmer working his own hundred acres go about
improving his "working conditions"? How was a small-town cobbler's,
grocer's, or tailor's situation different from that of the worker in

9 Dorothy S. Arnof, *A Sense of the Past* (New York: The Macmillan Company,
1962), p. 144.

Whitney's mill? The class might eventually understand, one hopes, that as America grew into an increasingly complex, industrial society the individual found himself less and less able to correct a great variety of problems purely "on his own"; he needed the cooperation of others, and he organized himself into effective, functioning groups.

The nature of a given society's political system and the nature of its political behavior are closely related to the fundamental system of values to which the society adheres.

The political behavior of a given society may be explained, as may its social behavior, in terms of its basic assumptions about the nature of the good life. Obviously, if a society believes that the dignity and worth of the individual human personality is of prime importance, that society will do its best to create a political system reflecting this fundamental value. Conversely, if a society believes that the nation or state must assume priority over individual persons, that society will develop a system upholding and reinforcing this ideal.

Although this third basic generalization appears to be exceedingly difficult for young children to comprehend, it might be grasped by upper-elementary-school pupils in various ways. For example, Bernard Asbell, an American educator who recently visited the Soviet Union, posed this question to a group of American ten-year-olds: "If you could be on Russian television for one minute and say anything you wanted, what do you think would be most important to say?" This is how they responded:

"I would tell them to have a mind of their own," said Judy. "If they hear things from their parents about how bad the U.S. is, I would tell them to try to find out for themselves."

Michael, the class president, said he would list a few things about American life: First, that no one tells you what to do; second, that no one tells you where to live—

Lynn interrupted his list. "But we don't really always let people live anywhere. We would have to be fair and tell the Russians about some bad things here, like about Negroes. Negroes here don't have equal rights in getting a house or in restaurants and buses, and we should be honest in telling about this."

Judy said, "I would like to ask what they think about our racial problem and find out how they treat Negroes."

"They don't have a problem," said Toby, "because they hardly have any Negroes, except visitors from Africa. They probably have different problems, like wheat."

The pupils burst into a discussion about the sale of American wheat to Russia. They wondered whether the Russian people had been told of their own wheat shortage, and if it was right to sell wheat. I polled the pupils. They believed that it was right to sell the Russians wheat.

"It wouldn't help our relationship not to," said Lynn. "They'd think we were very selfish."

"When you see them," said Robbie, "would you say that just because they're different, that doesn't mean we hate them. But frankly, we don't like them too much, because we think our way is right."

"Ask them," said Lynn, "why they think communism is better than democracy, because we might not know all the things that Khrushchev tells them."

I suggested that the Soviets might not understand our pitting the word "communism" against "democracy" as opposites; each of the countries that we call a Soviet satellite calls itself a "people's democratic republic." The pupils seemed shocked.

"Ask them," said Mark, "if they are surprised that we consider ourselves a democracy. I'm surprised that they call themselves one."

"Ask them," said Toby, "what they think we have for liberty, and what they want us to know they have."

"Ask them" said Robbie, "what they think freedom is." [10]

The teacher might ask the same question of his class, and/or he could read aloud or reproduce the responses of the children who were interviewed. In any case, the teacher and his class might look for words and phrases that are related to American values and ideals. Perhaps statements like the following would be made by pupils:

You should do what you think is right.
You should have a mind of your own.
We believe in freedom and justice for all.
All men should have equal rights.
We believe in being good sports, being fair.
We can go all over America and live where we want to.
It isn't good to be mean or selfish.

Building upon the responses of the students, the teacher might next attempt to outline with the class the kind of laws and government they might want *if* they really believed in these things and wanted to live accordingly.

The class might be interested in the way Russian children responded to some other related questions:

---

[10] Bernard Asbell, "What American and Russian Children Think of Each Other," *Redbook*, Vol. 123, No. 6 (October, 1964), 52–53.

"Freedom," said eight-year-old Alexei, "means that a man is not in chains. He works not for a landlord or rich person, but for his own country."

"Under freedom every man has a place to work."

"A free man doesn't have to depend on anyone."

. . . .

I found myself wondering whether these Russian children sounded so much alike because the same person was translating for all of them or because they were so much alike. When I brought this subject up one morning, Valery [a Russian guide] remarked that Americans he meets seem so different from one another. "In the Soviet Union," he said, "we try to be more the same." [11]

Perhaps the class might attempt to compare its responses with those of both groups quoted by Asbell and, at their level of maturity, discuss the similarities and differences in positions.

Another possibility for exploring *means-ends* connections between specific forms of behavior and democratic values and ideals involves the use of a group of brief news items. A high-school teacher could gather and mimeograph copies of stories such as these for students in his senior problems class:

One item might describe the orderly passage of a bill by the United States Senate.

A second story could deal with the owner of a business who has told his employees that they may vote for the candidate of their choice in a coming election but that he will give every employee a cash bonus if a given person is elected.

A third report might discuss the treatment a public speaker supporting the United Nations received from a group of "America-First" hecklers and demonstrators in a large public assembly.

Next, there might be a story about a group of college students running a free taxi service from an old-people's home to a precinct voting station.

The fifth account might cover illegal voter-registration procedures—through the use of addresses for vacant lots, abandoned buildings, etc.—employed by machine politicians in a given political party.

Another piece might announce an open city-council meeting which citizens owning property in a given area were invited to attend.

---

[11] *Ibid.*, pp. 53, 112.

Also, there might be an item concerning the withdrawal of white children by their parents from a newly integrated school.

The students might be asked to rank the news items from "most to least democratic" in approach. A lively discussion of democratic aims and methods could grow out of the reading and hierarchical arrangement of the items provided by the teacher.

The values upon which a given political system rests may be explored in an even more explicit manner. Ralph Henry Gabriel, professor emeritus of history at Yale University, was asked in 1963 to carry out a unique assignment for UNESCO. In effect, Professor Gabriel was requested to develop (with the help of a committee of distinguished scholars) a statement dealing with traditional values in American life. It was hoped that this statement might help other societies to understand and appreciate more fully the values upon which our system is based. Eventually, similar statements are to be produced by other nations, providing a basis for comparative study. Professor Gabriel's comprehensive statement can serve as a stimulating springboard for discussion of the relationship between traditional American values and the political system under which we live. It would seem, for example, that excerpts from the Gabriel statement might be compared with newspaper clippings dealing with actual events occurring in our society. For example, the following testimony (given in a Congressional hearing by the author of a proposed constitutional amendment which is designed to nullify the Supreme Court's recent prayer and Bible reading decisions) might be placed on one side of a bulletin board: "Millions of families do not subscribe to *any* religion. The children of such families are not aware of the existence of God. As part of their education for life the schools must make them aware." [12] Next to an item or group of items of this nature, the teacher could place these statements from the Gabriel Commission's report on American values: ". . . the values of religion in American life . . . include the following concepts: The freedom to believe . . . as the conscience of the individual person directs, or freedom to refrain from worship. . . ." [13]

Similarly, a clipping concerning the exclusion of a Negro from a given housing area or job might be compared with this value statement from the Gabriel report: "The social values of the American people [include] freedom, and so far as possible equal opportunity

---

[12] *Minneapolis Morning Tribune*, April 23, 1964, p. 14.
[13] Ralph Henry Gabriel, *Traditional Values in American Life* (New York: Harcourt, Brace & World, Inc., 1963), p. 13.

of the individual person to make of his life what he can in accordance with his abilities . . . the expectation of a status in society that derives from his qualities and achievements." [14]

What is the relationship betwen the two Gabriel Commission statements and the two news items? What are the implications for our society of the values stated by Gabriel? Most high-school teachers should find Gabriel's work exceedingly useful in bringing out into the open the relationship between a society's professed values and its political and social way of life. To, gain even more insight into Professor Gabriel's frame of reference, teachers who are not already familiar with this classic source should read *The Course of American Democratic Thought.*[15]

Statements by a variety of writers across the centuries can reveal some interesting approaches, stated and implied, to relationships between aims and political systems or schemes. With sufficient background and clarification of purpose, some individual high-school students might be encouraged to read such works as Plato's *Republic,* Aristotle's *Politics,* Machiavelli's *The Prince,* Rousseau's *The Social Contract,* Paine's *Common Sense,* Marx's and Engels' *The Communist Manifesto,* Hoover's *American Individualism,* Hitler's *Mein Kampf,* Dewey's *Freedom and Culture,* Becker's *Modern Democracy,* Malinowski's *Freedom and Civilization,* Orwell's *Animal Farm,* Smith and Lindeman's *The Democratic Way of Life,* Lippmann's *The Public Philosophy,* and Goldwater's *The Conscience of a Conservative.*[16]

---

[14] *Ibid.*

[15] *Idem, The Course of American Democratic Thought* (New York: The Ronald Press Company, 1956).

[16] These works are available in the following editions: Justin D. Kaplan (ed.), *Dialogues of Plato* (New York: Pocket Books, Inc., 1950); Justin D. Kaplan (ed.), *The Pocket Aristotle* (New York: The Pocket Library, 1950); Niccolo Machiavelli, *The Prince* (New York: New American Library of World Literature, Inc., 1952); Jean Jacques Rousseau, *The Social Contract and Discourses* (London: J. M. Dent and Sons, Ltd., 1947); Thomas Paine, *Common Sense* and *The Crisis* (Garden City, N.Y.: Doubleday & Company, 1960); Karl Marx and Friedrich Engels, *The Communist Manifesto* (New York: International Publishers Co., Inc., 1948); Herbert Hoover, *American Individualism* (Garden City, N.Y.: Doubleday & Company, 1922); Adolf Hitler, *Mein Kampf* (Boston: Houghton Mifflin Company, 1943); John Dewey, *Freedom and Culture* (New York: G. P. Putnam's Sons, 1939); Carl L. Becker, *Modern Democracy* (New Haven, Conn.: Yale University Press, 1941); Bronislaw Malinowski, *Freedom and Civilization* (New York: Roy Publishers, Inc., 1944); George Orwell, *Animal Farm* (New York: New American Library of World Literature, Inc., 1946); T. V. Smith and Eduard C. Lindeman, *The Democratic Way of Life* (New York: New American Library of World Literature, Inc., 1951); Walter Lippmann, *The Public Philosophy* (New York: New American Library of World Literature, Inc., 1956); Barry Goldwater, *The Conscience of a Conservative* (New York: Macfadden-Bartell Corp., 1960).

Some of the references are classic, others are not. Some are scholarly, others are not. Some are well grounded, others are not. It is to be hoped, however, that in reading them students would be stimulated to think about some vital issues. They would be dealing with ideas as expressed by their authors instead of with the usual bland, matter-of-fact, hasty, second-hand summaries found in a number of textbooks. If students could not read entire works, they might search in given books for material on single themes or issues such as freedom, equality, justice, the role of the state or nation, the nature of leadership, and so on. Or, the teacher might read to his class from a number of works on a topic or two.

The relationship between a set of goals and a political system can be ennobling, moral, beautiful, and positively directed. Yet, unfortunately, there is also a possibility that societal ends and political means can be degrading, immoral, ugly, and negatively directed. Below are some chilling excerpts from letters written by scientists at the I. G. Farben Chemical Company in Germany during World War II. They were addressed to the authorities at the infamous Auschwitz concentration camp. Perhaps these stark passages would give mature students a feeling for what can happen when objectives and political structure go awry.

> In contemplation of experiments with a new soporific drug, we would appreciate you procuring for us a number of women.

> We received your answer but consider the price of 200 marks a woman excessive. We propose to pay not more than 170 marks a head. If agreeable, we will take possession of the women. We need approximately 150.

> We acknowledge your accord. Prepare for us 150 women in the best possible health conditions, and as soon as you advise us you are ready, we will take charge of them.

> Received the order of 150 women. Despite their emaciated condition, they were found satisfactory. We shall keep you posted on developments concerning this experiment.

> The tests were made. All subjects died. We shall contact you shortly on the subject of a new load.[17]

The teacher might ask the class of high-school juniors or seniors to examine what kind of political orientation would have permitted

[17] Bruno Bettelheim, *The Informed Heart* (New York: The Free Press of Glencoe, Inc., 1960), pp. 247–48.

such unbelievable behavior. The students might analyze more carefully the democratic ideology in terms of its safeguards against this sort of occurrence. They could be asked whether this kind of practice could take place in the United States and whether they can document, support, clarify, and illustrate their responses to the question.

Political ideals, values, attitudes, and institutions develop and change over time.

Political systems in general and American democracy in particular have been subject to continuous developments and changes over the years. In some systems, political change has taken place in a gradual, orderly, evolutionary manner; whereas in others abrupt, often violent, revolutionary change has been the pattern. It seems fair to say, however, that there is no political system that has not been touched by time (for better or for worse).

We feel that it is particularly important for the citizens of our democracy to understand that American political ideals, institutions, perceptions, and practices are not static. The constitution has been interpreted and reinterpreted at different times in our history to meet the unique problems and challenges that arise from one generation to another. Similarly, our concept of the role of the presidency and the courts has undergone changes. It would be difficult indeed, in *any* reasonably honest approach to the study of the development of American political ideals and institutions, to avoid dealing with these changes. Teachers may find that the following approaches offer particularly promising opportunities to develop the concept of political change.

Junior- and senior-high-school teachers might read this account of the political activities of John Lilburne, a courageous seventeenth-century Englishman, to their students:

> When he was still a very young man, apprenticed to a merchant in the cloth trade in London, John Lilburne made a trip to Holland and, on his return, was arrested and haled before the Court of Star Chamber on suspicion of having smuggled "factious and scandalous" books into England. The suspicion was probably very well grounded. But Lilburne, who had learned a little law, insisted that no free Englishman could be compelled to answer questions except in response to specific charges and could not be required to serve as a witness against himself.
>
> For this, Lilburne was fined £500, a staggering sum for a young apprentice, was tied to a cart and, his body bared, was whipped

through the streets of London all the way from the Fleet prison to the Palace Yard at Westminster. And all the way, as the cart moved along and the lash fell upon him, John Lilburne, blessing God for having called him to his service, declaimed to the crowd about his wrongs and their rights.

At Westminster, he was placed in a pillory, bowed down with his back to the sun; and there he stood for two hours cheerfully exhorting all who would listen to resist the tyranny of the bishops. When he was told to be quiet, he refused; and so he was gagged, so cruelly that his mouth bled. And then, in a gesture as magnificent as it was theatrical, he plucked from the folds of his robe three copies of the pamphlet that had caused all the controversy and flung them to the crowd.

After this, Lilburne was thrown into the Fleet prison—for ten days in solitary confinement with irons on his hands and legs and with nothing to eat. For two and a half years he remained in prison—until at last the Long Parliament set him free.[18]

It would appear that an analysis of the political overtones attending Lilburne's actions—together with a comparison of the Lilburne case with current legal guarantees and processes—would be a stimulating classroom endeavor. The much misunderstood, sometimes misused and maligned, fifth amendment to our constitution provides a topical and significant problem for older students to investigate. Newspapers and magazines have described many instances in which the fifth amendment has been taken by those being investigated for a variety of purposes. These same publications sometimes have carried statements by columnists, editors, and writers of letters to the editor which condemned the very amendment itself. After careful study of the amendment, its purpose, the freedoms it guarantees, and its application over the years, students might role-play a group of political situations. In one incident, the class might assume that the fifth amendment has not been written and does not exist. Each of the actors in this political drama might be given beforehand a slip of paper which provides some background information and sets the scene; for example:

Young Man

You are an alert, outgoing person who enjoys life and gets along well with people. You have high ideals, respect and obey the law, and have the courage to defend what is right and to "stick to your guns." You finished high school last year, and you

---

[18] Alan Barth, "The Levellers and Civil Liberties," *Civil Liberties*, No. 214, March, 1964, p. 2.

are now employed as a stock clerk in a large department store. You may try to go to college next year. After work tonight, you decided to stay downtown for a bite of food and a movie. It is now close to midnight. You are waiting for the Second Avenue bus going east. This is a depressed section of town, and the streets are deserted with the exception of a man across the street who is waiting for a west-bound bus. It is a chilly night, and you step back in a doorway to get out of the wind. A man startles you by rushing up and asking for a cigarette. You reply that you do not smoke and ask him if he knows what time it is. He mumbles something and hurries off.

First Policeman

You are an impatient, hot-tempered, belligerent individual. You have few friends, even among your fellow officers. You are an insensitive, and occasionally cruel, person who dislikes his work and whose attitudes have been criticized by his superiors. Yesterday you were told that there are a growing number of narcotics-pushers working on your beat and that you should "wake up" and see if you can "do something" about this situation. As you walk your beat with another officer tonight, you happen to glance down the street in time to observe a young man enter a doorway and stand there. Your suspicions are aroused when a second person joins the first briefly and then rushes off. In the instant when the second man steps out of the doorway, his face is illuminated by the street light. You recognize him as a known local drug addict who was involved in a fight on your beat about a month ago. "This is it!" you think. "The man in the doorway must be a pusher! He must be a really cool operator to sell stuff out in the open like this! Here is my chance to get one of 'em and to get in good with Sergeant Brady and Lieutenant Simpson! I'll show Brady and Simpson who's awake! I'll not only nab the guy, but I'll wrap up the whole deal tonight. If I can't find any dope on him, I'll *make* him confess anyway!" You hurry toward the suspect.

Second Policeman

You are a relaxed, easy-going, relatively weak person. You can be swayed and led easily by a strong, dominating individual. You have been a patrolman for ten years with only minimum salary boosts and no promotion. You have a wife and four children, and things are very close financially at home. You have received considerable pressure from your superiors to "crack down" on narcotics pushers who are increasingly active on your beat. An arrest or two would look good on your record and could help your status and your income. All of this is running through your mind as you walk your rounds with your partner. He nudges you suddenly so you will see a young man step into a doorway. You keep your eyes on the young man and then see someone else approach the doorway. The men in the doorway are together briefly, and then the second man comes away from the first quickly. A street light shines on the second man's face for just a moment, and you immediately identify him as an addict who was in trouble a few weeks before. The second man disappears in the darkness. Your partner's pace quickens, and you know he is thinking the same thing you are.

The sociodrama might be enacted by just one group or by a second and even a third one if fruitful comments emerge. If it is enacted a second or third time, the teacher might alter the descriptions of the participants, add or subtract a character, or change the action. Discussion would be led to center on a comparison of the sociodrama with John Lilburne's experience. Students should perceive that without the fifth amendment, people *could* now be treated much as Lilburne was. The gradual *development* of many of our current political beliefs and guarantees dealing with such things as arresting procedures; the rights, treatment, and questioning of the suspect; and the proper gathering and handling of evidence grew out of protests like Lilburne's. Compelling innocent men to confess to crimes they had not committed and convict themselves out of their own mouths was once common practice. Time has given us opportunities to originate, refine, and polish guarantees of political freedom; and life *without* them would probably be dangerous, insecure, and bleak indeed.

Possibly even upper-elementary-school children could partially understand and begin to evaluate the birth, growth, and maturation of political values and ideals through carefully selected material and individually tailored methods. Teachers dealing with early American colonial life, for example, might attempt to discuss the implications of the following official court record describing the fate of Wenlock Christison, arrested and tried in Boston in 1661 for the crime of being a Quaker:

. . . At the . . next General-Court, Wenlock Christison was again brought to the Bar.

The Governour asked him, "What he had to say for himself, why he should not die?"

Wenlock: I have done nothing worthy of Death. . . .

Court: We have a Law, and by our Law you are to die. . . .

Wenlock: Are you Subjects to the King, yea, or nay? . . .

Court: Yes.

Wenlock: So am I, and for anything I know, am as good as you, if not better; for if the King did but know your Hearts are as rotten towards Him, as they are towards God. Therefore seeing that you and I are Subjects to the King, I demand to be tried by the Laws of my own Nation.

Court: You shall be tried by . . . a Jury

Wenlock: That is not the Law, but the Manner of it for if you will be as good as your Word, you must set me at Liberty, for I never heard or read of any Law to hang Quakers. . . .

Court: You are in our Hand, and have broken our Laws, and we will try you.

Wenlock: . . . Jury, take heed what you do . . . Look for your Evidence: What have I done to deserve Death? Keep your Hands out of innocent Blood. . . .

The Jury went out, but . . . soon returned, and brought in their Verdict Guilty.

Wenlock: I deny all Guilt, for my Conscience is clear in the Sight of God.

Governour: The Jury hath condemned thee. . . .

Wenlock: It were better for thee to be at Home than here, for thou art about a bloody piece of Work.

Governour: . . . Wenlock Christison, hearken to your Sentence: You must return unto the Place from whence you came, and from thence to the Place of Execution, and there you must be hanged until you be dead, dead, dead, upon the 13th Day of June, being the Fifth-day of the Week. . . . Take him away. . . .[19]

The class could be asked to discuss *why* the Boston court punished Quakers so severely. Other illustrations of religious intolerance during the colonial period might also be employed. Eventually, the teacher might lead his class to the conclusion that freedom of religion meant different things to different people during our past and that the concept as we know it today was modified through the years.

In another, but related, vein, the office of the presidency itself has changed drastically over time. Older students could develop specific and detailed comparisons, but even relatively young children may gain some feeling for the alterations in the office through documents such as those below. The first describes a typical day during

---

[19] A. B. Hart, *American History Told by Contemporaries* (New York: The Macmillan Co., 1908), pp. 481–84.

the administration of President Washington. The second reports one of Lyndon Johnson's average days

Thursday, 18th.
1790

Sat for Mr. Trumbull from 9 o'clock till 10: after which exercised in the post-chaise with Mrs. Washington. On our return home called on Mrs. Adams, lady of the Vice-President.

The following company dined here today, viz:—Judge Cushing and his lady: the Postmaster General and his lady: and Messers. Boudinot, Griffin, Coles, Gerry, and White, and their ladies.

Sent a message to the Senate with the copies of a letter from the Governor of Massachusetts, and a resolve of the Assembly of that State respecting the disputed boundary between them and the British of Nova Scotia.

THE WHITE HOUSE [20]
WASHINGTON
Tuesday, April 21, 1964

7:15 A.M.	Reading of newspapers and reports
8:40	Downstairs to join Legislative Leaders
8:45	LEGISLATIVE LEADERS BREAKFAST
	.
	.
	.
9:30	President arrived in the office (President's office) with Legislative Leaders
	Telephone calls*
11:05	Address in Rose Garden before a group of Treasury agency heads, their deputies, personnel officers and deputy employment policy officers on civil rights and fair employment practices (approximately 60 people)
11:15	Meeting with: Hon. C. Douglas Dillon, Secretary of Treasury
	Hon. Henry Fowler

---

* (President received and placed approximately 27 telephone calls in the course of the day.)

---

[20] "The President's Day," *American Heritage*, Vol. 15, No. 5 (August, 1964), 106–7.

11:35	The President received the members of the Public Advisory Committee for Trade Negotiations (approximately 35 people). Made informal remarks.
11:55	Received representatives of the DISCIPLES OF CHRIST HISTORICAL SOCIETY in his office. (The group [about 12] presented the President with a lifetime membership in the Society and a booklet)
12:05 P.M.	The President went to the Rose Garden to address the Editors and Broadcasters (approximately 200) in connection with the Semi-Annual National Foreign Policy Conference
12:40	The President returned to his office with Robert Manning, Assistant Secretary of State for Public Affairs
	Telephone calls
12:50	Met with Dean Rusk and McGeorge Bundy who remained through lunch
12:55	Received Governor and Mrs. John Connally of Texas
1:20	To Mansion for lunch with Hon. Dean Rusk
	Hon. Robert McNamara
	Hon. McGeorge Bundy
2:45	Telephone calls
5:01	President returned to office
5:10	President met with Congressman Mendel Rivers
	Telephone calls and conferences with staff members
5:45	Meeting with H. E. Romulo Betancourt (former president of Venezuela) and H. E. Dr. Enrique Tejera-Paris, Ambassador of Venezuela
6:21	Meeting with Hon. Ernest W. McFarland
6:50 to 8:45	President met with staff members and received and placed telephone calls
8:45	Signed mail
9:10	Departed office and went to the Mansion
9:20	Dinner with Mrs. Johnson
10:13	Met with Hon. Robert McNamara

For years, millions of Americans took it for granted that slavery was both legal and just, that there was no need for women to vote, that it was all right for little children to work long hours at hard labor, and so forth. The following argument against free public schools, published in the Philadelphia *National Gazette* in 1830, could be used effectively by the teacher at a number of grade levels in his attempt to dramatize changes in attitudes toward governmental responsibilities:

> It is an old and sound remark that government cannot provide for the necessities of the People; it is they who maintain the government, and the latter the People. Education may be among their necessities; but it is one which the State or national councils cannot supply. . . . To create schools for all classes—is beyond their power. Education in general must be the work of the intelligence, need, and enterprise of individuals and associations. . . . Some of the writers about universal public instruction and discipline, seem to forget the constitution. . . .[21]

A more sophisticated and complex problem that illustrates the evolvement of an ideal has to do with the desegregation of our nation's schools. Excerpts from the Supreme Court's historic decision might be carefully explored by high-school students. In particular, they should be asked to outline the Court's arguments for *changing* the "separate but equal" position which had been in effect for sixty years. The following excerpts from *Brown* versus *Board of Education* (May 17, 1954) may provide the raw material for such an exercise:

> Today, education is perhaps the most important function of state and local governments. It is required in the performance of our most basic public responsibilities, even service in the armed forces. It is the very foundation of good citizenship. In these days, it is doubtful that any child may reasonably be expected to succeed in life if he is denied the opportunity of an education. Such an opportunity, where the state has undertaken to provide it, is a right which must be made available to all on equal terms.
> . . . To separate children from others of similar age and qualifications solely because of their race generates a feeling of inferiority as to their status in the community that may affect their hearts and minds in a way unlikely ever to be undone. . . .
> We conclude that in the field of public education the doctrine of "separate but equal" has no place. Separate educational facilities are inherently unequal.[22]

Political change can also be demonstrated vividly through the use of political cartoons. Allan Nevins' *A Century of Political Car-*

---

[21] Allan Nevins, *American Press Opinion* (New York: D. C. Heath & Company, 1928), p. 81.
[22] Harold Syrett, *American Historical Documents* (New York: Barnes & Noble, Inc., 1960), pp. 409–12.

toons [23] is filled with examples of American political values, attitudes, and perceptions from 1800 through 1902. Although dozens of topics might be discussed, it would be particularly useful to use material indicating changing views of leading political figures over the years. For example, Abraham Lincoln, who is held in almost universal esteem today, was not always seen in this light. The cartoon called "Running the Machine" attacks both the Lincoln administration in general and Lincoln personally.[24] For many students, the idea that famous political figures of the past were often vilified and roundly criticized is a new political insight. Many of today's students tend to view the heroes of the past as godlike personages—men who were faultless, omniscient, and omnipotent. A corollary of this view is that modern leaders do not measure up to those of the past and that if only a hero in the traditional pattern would emerge, our troubles would soon be over. This unrealistic way of looking at political leaders can be modified without in any way degrading great men of the past.

Finally, teachers and students alike might gain a deeper sense of the kinds of change we have been discussing through pondering Bertrand Russell's poignant reminiscence at the age of 90:

> For those who are too young to remember the world before 1914, it must be difficult to imagine the contrast for a man of my age between childhood memories and the world of the present day. I try, though with indifferent success, to accustom myself to a world of crumbling empires, Communism, atom bombs, Asian self-assertion, and aristocratic downfall. In this strange insecure world where no one knows whether he will be alive tomorrow, and where ancient states vanish like morning mists, it is not easy for those who, in youth, were accustomed to ancient solidities to believe that what they are now experiencing is a reality and not a transient nightmare. Very little remains of institutions and ways of life that when I was a child appeared as indestructible as granite.[25]

In every society, individuals and groups disagree over some societal goals and directions, over how aims will be achieved, and over the enforcement of standards of behavior.

Political conflict exists to some extent in every society. There are varying degrees of disagreement even in totalitarian situations, as one

---

[23] New York: Charles Scribner's Sons, 1944.
[24] *A Century of Political Cartoons*, pp. 108–9.
[25] Bertrand Russell, *The Basic Writings of Bertrand Russell* (New York: Simon and Schuster, 1961), p. 51.

can observe from ancient times to the present (for example, the internal strife at the top in the U.S.S.R. in 1964 which led to Khruschev's replacement by Kosygin and Brezhnev). Some societies have tried to stamp out, avoid, or overlook variances in opinions and to impose a monistic "consensus"; but the existence of divergent views is to be expected, encouraged, and welcomed with open arms in a pluralistic society. The statement, "I disapprove of what you say, but I will defend to the death your right to say it," attributed to Voltaire, is laden with meaning for democrats. So, also are the ideas of "Her Majesty's loyal opposition." Political conflict exists in our country and should be acknowledged, understood, and appreciated. In many instances, our schools in particular have tried to side-step or gloss over controversy and contrasting points of view. Some of the crucial issues that face the American citizen today have been left virtually unexplored. In this all too brief section, we shall attempt to suggest a few practical classroom methods teachers could employ in an effort to explore with young people the idea of political conflict. The techniques which follow are intended, first, to make the student aware of the fact that divergence of opinion does exist in America and, second, to help him better comprehend the positions themselves and their implications.

The teacher might choose to open this area of investigation through the use of a political-attitudes or -values test similar to those developed by Remmers and Radler in *The American Teenager*. The authors have devoted many years to studying the opinions of high-school students, and their book contains a wide variety of discussion-stimulating ideas. The following sample test items, for example, could be used to explore individual attitudes toward a number of problems directly related to the American political scene:

Indicate Whether You Agree, Disagree or Are Uncertain
About the Following Statement

——If a person is uncertain how to vote, it is better if he does not vote.

——Pressure groups are useful and important features of representative government.

——Communism and Fascism are basically the same.

——The most serious danger to democracy in the United States comes from Communists and Communist-dominated groups.

——There should be more women in public office.

——The average citizen is justified in remaining aloof from dirty politics that may exist in his community.[26]

The teacher might have the class write their reasons for agreeing or disagreeing with a given statement. Various arguments can be recorded, categorized, or quantified; and the class ought to gain a better understanding of the divergent opinions held by the many individuals who make up the group.

Teachers working with young people from the intermediate through the senior-high-school levels may make use of the material published in the letters-to-the-editor column of any good newspaper. This approach yields particularly fruitful results during an election campaign. Over a specified period of time, the class can clip out those letters that are politically partisan, list and classify the various arguments presented, and so forth. The purpose here would be to demonstrate the spectrum of political opinion held by an area's citizens rather than to evaluate each argument.

Another promising approach to the recognition of political conflict and its implications involves the creation of an hypothetical political figure—let us say, Senator Howe Willie Vote. The Senator would be, in a sense, a sort of computor into which the class could feed a variety of personal and political data. To start, the class might organize personal information about Senator Vote, such as the following: (1) home state and place of residence within that state (urban or rural, large or small city, etc.); (2) age; (3) educational background; (4) former occupation and occupation of parents; (5) nature of immediate family; (6) financial status; (7) membership in religious, professional, business, political, and social organizations and groups; (8) political party and possible faction within that party; (9) past political experience, seniority in the Senate, and committee and other special assignments; and (10) over-all patterns in voting record. The ingredients in the Senator's make-up can be very simple or quite complex, depending upon the ability and interests of students in a given class.

Having assembled a set of personal components, the class would be ready next to place Howe Willie Vote into a specific voting situation. A bill currently being considered, previously handled, or yet to come before Congress would be selected. Students would be given as much information as they could handle and assimilate about the nature of the bill, some of its announced proponents and opponents, etc. Then, each student would place himself in the Senator's shoes and decide how he would vote. The decision might be an "easy," rather

---

[26] H. H. Remmers and D. H. Radler, *The American Teenager* (Indianapolis, Ind.: The Bobbs-Merrill Co., Inc., 1957).

obvious, one in which most of the class members could agree on how they think their imaginary politician would respond. If this is the case the first time around, one significant factor in the Senator's background might be altered to produce possible conflict. For instance, his residence could be changed from one state to another or from a large industrial city to a small farm town; or he could be given membership in the Sons of the American Revolution or the National Association for the Advancement of Colored People, or the American Federation of Labor. The teacher should keep in mind that this approach is not intended to induce stereotypic, either/or thinking, nor is it expected to possess precision or surety. No one knows exactly what effect *any* of Senator Vote's personal characteristics, affiliations, or alliances—taken singly or placed in various combinations—might have in reality; but students would surely see that an individual may face political conflicts in his own make-up as well as in his contacts with others. Political conflict is inevitable in our heterogeneous, democratic nation. Our task as citizens is to try to understand such conflict and why it exists, to learn to capture with increased accuracy the frame of reference of another individual, to perfect the capacity to accept other human beings as persons of dignity and worth whether we agree with their views or not, and to discover more and more ways of building unity with diversity.

Another means of illustrating political conflict could involve the collection of contrasting editorials or other published opinions from different periods of time, areas of the United States, philosophical orientations, and so forth. For example, editorials from Southern and Northern newspapers might be compared in the editions immediately following the Supreme Court's desegregation decision of 1954 or the passage of the Civil Rights Act of 1964. Columnists such as James Reston and David Lawrence might be compared on any number of issues, as might newspapers such as the liberal *Washington Post* and the more conservative *New York Herald-Tribune*. Given adequate library facilities or good copying equipment, the teacher might expose his students to contemporary expressions of conflicting opinion on issues such as America's membership in the United Nations, involvement in Korea, and so on.

The teacher might help students examine the idea of political conflict in other, less topical, ways as well. For example, high-school students might pretend they are newspaper reporters covering political beats. They would be asked to write up imaginary interviews, on many controversial issues, with former Presidents, Cabinet members, senators, Supreme Court Justices, ambassadors, and others all the way back to the birth of our nation. Some men, who lived during different periods in American history or at the same time, could be paired on a particular issue; and for contrast, the two "reporters" could read their "interviews" together in front of the class. For instance, George Washington and Franklin Roosevelt could be asked about the issue of a third term; Daniel Webster and Robert Hayne, states' rights; Woodrow Wilson and Senator Henry Cabot Lodge, the League of Nations; Franklin Roosevelt and Robert A. Taft, TVA or Social Security; Joseph McCarthy and Hubert Humphrey, the internment of American citizens of Japanese ancestry during World War II or trade with Communist nations; and so on. Special emphasis would be placed on the sources of information used by each student, his objectivity, and his ability to identify with the person "interviewed."

Conflict exists in our society about the means of enforcing agreed-upon goals as well as about the goals themselves. For example, although the taking of another man's life is universally condemned by law, a debate over capital punishment has raged (and continues to rage) in many states. Fourteen states have voted to abolish the death penalty. Of the fourteen, however, ten have decided to restore it. What arguments have been given for and against capital punishment through the years? Have attitudes toward the death penalty changed over time? Which groups support it, and which attack it? Why? Jeanne Kuebler's little pamphlet, *Punishment by Death,*[27] summarizes arguments in a straightforward, objective manner and might be used by senior-high-school students as a convenient basis for study and discussion.

Similarly, controversy exists in some parts of the United States concerning both the enforcement of law and the administration of justice. *Is* every American equal before the law? Do some Americans believe in a *dual* system of justice? Should standards of behavior be enforced differently for different groups of Americans? Questions like these might well be triggered by a reading of a report similar to the following: "An all-white Birmingham jury in mid-January convicted a 16-year-old white youth of second-degree manslaughter in the slaying of a 13-year-old Negro boy last September after the church bombing that ended the lives of four girls at Sunday School; the white teenager was sentenced to seven months in the county jail." [28]

It should be pointed out here that the chief concern of the political-science-oriented teacher in studies such as these is not merely to illustrate what appears to be a miscarriage of justice, but rather to

---

[27] Washington, D.C.: Editorial Research Reports, 1156 Nineteenth Street, N. W., 1963.

[28] *Civil Liberties,* No. 214, March, 1964, p. 4.

encourage his students to seek explanations of such phenomena. *Why do these things happen?* What attitudes, values, and experiences lie behind behavior of this sort?

CONCLUSION

Peter Odegard once summarized the significance of behavioral science in general and political science in particular in these words:

> . . . men [must] choose among alternative modes of thought and behavior. It is in helping people to make these choices not as sheep but as men, not blindly in response to subliminal stimuli or visceral incitation but consciously and rationally that behavioral science can make its best contribution, knowing that human nature, no less than the physical universe about us, admits of scientific exploration and analysis, and—within limits—of guidance and control.[29]

We hope that this book has helped its readers toward a more rational understanding of the nature of the political process. Although no single volume can deal exhaustively with the complex field of political science, we trust that some of the basic concepts and insights of the discipline have been clarified and brought to life in these pages.

---

[29] Peter Odegard, "Values and Their Communication" (Unpublished position paper, October, 1962), p. 7.

INDEX

INDEX